JESSICA HARPER

the

DISCOVERING **WHO** YOU ARE

Identity

AND **WHY** YOU ARE HERE.

project

A 40 DAY JOURNEY

Ark House Press
PO Box 1722, Port Orchard, WA 98366 USA
PO Box 1321, Mona Vale NSW 1660 Australia
PO Box 318 334, West Harbour, Auckland 0661 New Zealand
arkhousepress.com

© Jessica Harper

All rights reserved. No part of this publication may be reproduced, stored in a retrieval system or transmitted in any form or by any means electronic, mechanical, photocopying, recording or otherwise without the prior written permission of the publisher.

Scripture quotations taken from The Holy Bible, New International Version ©, NIV©, Copyright © 1973, 1978, 1984, 2011 by Biblica, Inc. © Used by permission. All rights reserved worldwide.

Cataloguing in Publication Data:
Title: The Identity Project
ISBNs: 978-0-6486703-7-7 (pbk.)
Subjects: Devotional; Journal; Christian;
Other Authors/Contributors: Harper, Jessica

Photography by www.NatashaBeaumont.com
Design by initiateagency.com

For Charlie and Josh. May you always know how loved, valued and uniquely gifted you are.

And to the many women in my life who have helped me to see my identity from Heaven's perspective. I am forever grateful that God has blessed me with your friendship.

Contents

Day 1:	Welcome	1
Day 2:	Your Passport To Purpose	7
Day 3:	The Identity Issue	13
Day 4:	A Solid Rock To Build On	19
PART ONE:	**MARKED BY THE MARKER**	**27**
Day 5:	God Doesn't Make Mistakes	28
Day 6:	The Seven Marks Of The Maker	35
Day 7:	You Are A Spiritual Being	41
Day 8:	You Are Creative	48
Day 9:	You Are Intelligent	54
Day 10:	You Communicate	60
Day 11:	You Are Relational	66
Day 12:	You Have A Moral Compass	72
Day 13:	You Have A Sense Of Purpose	78
Day 14:	Fallen With The Chance To Be Fully Restored	85
PART TWO	**FOUND IN FAMILY**	**93**
Day 15:	The Born Again Identity	94
Day 16:	Found In Family	101
Day 17:	You Were Predestined	105
Day 18:	You Have Been Chosen	112
Day 19:	You Have Been Redeemed	119
Day 20:	You Have Been Justified	126
Day 21:	You Have Been Adopted	132
Day 22:	You Are Royal	139

Day 23:	You Have An Inheritance	146
Day 24:	You Are Called	153
Day 25:	You Are Empowered	159
Day 26:	I Can Do All Things	166

PART THREE	GIFTED FOR GREATNESS	173
Day 27:	Stir It Up	174
Day 28:	Your Personality	180
Day 29:	Your Love Language	187
Day 30:	Your Spiritual Gifts	194
Day 31:	Your Skills, Talents & Passions	201

PART FOUR	POSITIONED FOR PURPOSE	209
Day 32:	Putting The Pieces In Place	210
Day 33:	Discovering Purpose	217
Day 34:	Write It Down	224
Day 35:	Pearls & Pigs	231

PART FIVE	BUILDING HEALTHY HABITS	239
Day 36:	Reading The Word	240
Day 37:	Prayer	247
Day 38:	Worship	254
Day 39:	Hearing God's Voice	261
Day 40:	Go & Live Loved!	270

| Thank you | 275 |
| References | 277 |

DAY 1:

WELCOME

*'He has made everything beautiful in its time.
He has also set eternity in the human heart.'
Ecclesiastes 3:11 NIV*

You are created for great things. You have been put here on Earth right here and right now for significance. There is nothing about who you are that is accidental and certainly nothing about you that is a mistake. Regardless of what you have been told or believed about your life, the truth is that you have been carefully and masterfully put together by a Father in Heaven who loves you and has a great plan for you!

The only problem is that very few of us dare to believe this truth, much less live every day and make every decision from this perspective… But we should.

My one goal in writing this journal is that you would begin to build your life from this place: from a place of true identity and from a place that truly understands just how intimately loved, uniquely gifted and incredibly valued you are. My hope is that you would wake each morning from a place that begins to dream wild dreams and chase the deepest desires of your heart, from a place of significance and a place that longs to see others flourish and bloom in life… Because this, my friend, is actually the life you have been created to live.

Does something flutter in your heart as your read these words? Do they challenge some part of you? Does hope begin to stir in your spirit? I pray that it does because there is something inside each of us that longs to live from this place. There is something in each of our hearts that longs to make a difference, to achieve something significant, to leave a mark of lasting change in this life. Do you feel it?

I love how King Solomon, the author of Ecclesiastes, identifies this stirring as the pull of eternity, which God Himself has set in each one of our hearts. For it is, in fact, our Creator who has placed within each of us this great desire for meaning and purpose, and a drive to discover what that might be for each of our lives. We see this reflected in so many ways, particularly when we find ourselves asking questions like:
'Who am I?'
'Why am I here?' or
'Is there a greater purpose to my existence than what I can see?'

People have asked questions like this for thousands of years and many a philosopher, doctor, psychologist, astrologer and insightful thinker have attempted to provide answers to them. But the truth is that these questions can only be answered truly and fully by the God who placed them in our hearts, and that is the journey I invite you to take over the next 40 days.

I will warn you up front that this journey may be a little uncomfortable. We are going to explore in detail the hidden corners of our hearts. This journey may force you to be open and vulnerable about areas of your life that have been suffocated or strangled by lies about who you are. But I know that if you are willing to dig deep with the Holy Spirit over these few weeks, He longs to uproot the lies that you have believed about your identity and plant a glorious, blooming garden of truth and life in your heart instead. Will you embark on this journey with me?

PAUSE, PONDER, REFLECT

Questions to Reflect on:
Have you ever considered the thought that a master plan is already laid out for your life? That God has already planned the absolute best version of your future? What thoughts and feelings come to mind when you consider this possibility?

Scriptures to ponder:

'For I know the plans I have for you," declares the Lord, "plans to prosper you and not to harm you, plans to give you hope and a future. Then you will call on me and come and pray to me, and I will listen to you. You will seek me and find me when you seek me with all your heart.'
Jeremiah 29:11-13 NIV

'He has made everything beautiful and appropriate in its time. He has also planted eternity [a sense of divine purpose] in the human heart [a mysterious longing which nothing under the sun can satisfy, except God]—yet man cannot find out (comprehend, grasp) what God has done (His overall plan) from the beginning to the end.'
Ecclesiastes 3:11 AMP

'Never doubt God's mighty power to work in you and accomplish all this. He will achieve infinitely more than your greatest request, your most unbelievable dream, and exceed your wildest imagination! He will out do them all, for his miraculous power constantly energizes you.' Ephesians 3:20 TPT

WELCOME

THE IDENTITY PROJECT

DAY 2:

YOUR PASSPORT TO PURPOSE

'God, investigate my life; get all the facts firsthand. I'm an open book to you; even from a distance, you know what I'm thinking.' Psalm 139:1-2 MSG

I'm so glad you are have decided to embark on this journey! As we begin, I want to spend some time thinking about purpose. So many people spend their lives looking for or pursuing purpose. We can define purpose as something bigger than ourselves; something worth getting out of bed for each day. If we are going to live a full life, it's so important that we find the unique purpose God has prepared for each of our lives.

So, as we take some time to focus on purpose today, I want you to imagine your purpose as a destination. Perhaps a land overseas, perhaps a place you would love to visit. Paris could be your place of purpose, or the wild wilderness of Canada, or the tropical beaches of Fiji. Imagine a place where life is exciting and challenging and rewarding and fulfilling all at once because you are living with purpose and with meaning.

Now, if you were going to travel to this place, you would require a passport, right? What is a passport? It is a document that proves who you are, a document that identifies you. It is only small and might not look very significant, however it has the power to take you where you want to go.

Now let me ask you this: how far would you get if you created a counterfeit passport? How far would you get if you tried to use somebody else's passport? Probably all the way to the office of the Federal Police! You most definitely wouldn't get where you wanted to go.

In the same way you require a passport to get to your destination when travelling overseas, I believe you need a passport to get to your place of purpose in this life. And just as a passport is a marker of *identity*, a reflection of *who you are*, your purpose passport is also a marker of identity, a reflection of how God sees you and hopefully the way you will come to see yourself.

Just as you cannot travel using someone else's passport, you cannot live a life of meaning and purpose trying to be somebody else. Once you get on that treadmill, you will never catch up! Trying to be somebody other than who God created you to be will only leave you exhausted and going nowhere. Trying to build your identity based on the expectations of others will produce the same result. Although it can be a daunting thought to consider, we must become fully comfortable in the fact that we are totally unique if we are going to discover our unique purpose in life. The truth is that there is no one else like you – just ask your fingerprints! It is only when we become confident and secure in *our own unique identity* that we can step into the life of meaning, purpose, destiny and fulfilment that we long for and that God has prepared for each of us. It is only through knowing and understanding *who we are* that true purpose is unlocked in our lives.

This journal is all about just that: building *your* identity and discovering *your* unique purpose. Not the person next to you, not the person you think you should be, not the person you have been told you should be, but the true you that God has handcrafted. We are going to start broad and dig deep, building layer upon layer, until hopefully you have a clear Christ-centred image of who you are, a firm foundation on which to build a life of meaning, purpose and significance!

A life of great purpose and fulfilment is waiting for you. Are you willing to pick up your unique passport and start moving towards it?

PAUSE, PONDER, REFLECT

Questions to Reflect on:
Take some time to honestly reflect on the current state of your identity. Is it built on the expectations of others? Are you pouring all your time and energy into looking or acting or being like somebody else, or do you see yourself the way God, your Creator, sees you? What kind of identity do you think will get you to the

place of purpose that God planned for your life? Will you make a decision today to partner with the truth of who God says you are when it comes to your identity?

Scriptures to ponder:

> 'The purposes of a person's heart are deep waters, but one who has insight draws them out.' Proverbs 20:5 NIV

> 'God's love is meteoric, His loyalty astronomic, His purpose titanic, His verdicts oceanic. Yet in his largeness nothing gets lost; Not a man, not a mouse, slips through the cracks.' Psalm 36:5-6 MSG

> 'So here's what I want you to do, God helping you: Take your everyday, ordinary life—your sleeping, eating, going-to-work, and walking-around life—and place it before God as an offering. Embracing what God does for you is the best thing you can do for Him. Don't become so well-adjusted to your culture that you fit into it without even thinking. Instead, fix your attention on God. You'll be changed from the inside out. Readily recognize what He wants from you, and quickly respond to it. Unlike the culture around you, always dragging you down to its level of immaturity, God brings the best out of you, develops well-formed maturity in you.' Romans 12:1-2 MSG

YOUR PASSPORT TO PURPOSE

THE IDENTITY PROJECT

DAY 3:

THE IDENTITY ISSUE

'My frame was not hidden from you when I was made in the secret place, when I was woven together in the depths of the earth. Your eyes saw my unformed body.'
Psalm 139:15 NIV

Welcome to Day 3! I wanted to give you a bit of my own backstory today. You may be thinking 'Identity? Why write a whole book about this?' Great question. Put simply, I got to the point where I felt utterly compelled to write about it. About three years ago, the Holy Spirit prompted me to begin studying the Bible to unpack what it meant to be made *in the image of God*. (You might have heard this phrase before; it packs more punch than you realize.) This lead to another study on what it meant to be *in Christ* and some more reading and study on what it really means to be *uniquely created*. As I got further and further into reading and learning what the Word of God says about who we are – our identity – I began to see not only a huge gap between the truth I was reading and the way I lived my life, but an even bigger gap between the truth I was reading and the way society was suggesting we build our identity.

I began to see more and more just how much this area of our lives comes under attack and that when our identity is weak, or built on shaky foundations, every other area of our lives is affected. I remember countless times hearing stories of struggle or heartache or painful situations that people around me were going through and thinking 'all of the challenges you are facing really come out of the same core issue: deep down, you just don't really know who you are!'

You see, when you don't understand the value that your life has, when you don't understand your worth, and when you don't understand that you have been lovingly and uniquely created to fulfill a destiny that only you can, you will tolerate things in your life that should never be given a place. This happens in different ways for each of us. Maybe you put up with manipulative people around your life because you don't believe you are worthy of better friendships. Maybe you stay in a relationship that isn't healthy because you don't believe you deserve to be treated any better. Maybe you allow words that are said about you to sink in because you don't have any stronger truth to push them back with, or maybe you refuse to follow the dreams in your heart because fear of failure grips you. However the attack comes, I am sure that at some point in your life your identity has been challenged and perhaps come off second best at the end of the battle. But that can stop today! The damage can be repaired and your identity can be rebuilt through the light, life and love that God wants to bring into your heart as He shows you who you truly are.

I am fully convinced that if you knew the plan God has for your life, you wouldn't want to be anybody else. Imagine a plan that has been tailor-made to suit you perfectly, to use your strengths, to include the things you are passionate about and to outwork the deepest desires of your heart. If you could only get a glimpse of this plan, you wouldn't want to walk any other road than the one God has placed before you, and you wouldn't let fear or insecurity hold you back any longer.

And that, my friend, is the path we are setting out to find together, and the path on which you will find the fulfillment, meaning and purpose that your heart longs for. It is God's desire for you to begin to see yourself as He sees you and to walk in the fullness of all that He has planned out for you.

PAUSE, PONDER, REFLECT

Questions to Reflect on:
Consider the relationships around your life and place them before God. Are there any patterns or behaviours that you can see that indicate your identity is weak or broken? How do you think these relationships would look if you lived from a place that truly understood your worth and value?

Scriptures to ponder:
> 'So we are convinced that every detail of our lives is continually woven together to fit into God's perfect plan of bringing

good into our lives, for we are His lovers who have been called to fulfil His designed purpose.' Romans 8:28 TPT

*'God, I invite your searching gaze into my heart.
Examine me through and through;
find out everything that may be hidden within me.
Put me to the test and sift through all my anxious cares.
See if there is any path of pain I'm walking on,
and lead me back to your glorious, everlasting ways—
the path that brings me back to you.'
Psalm 139:23-24 TPT*

*'In Him also we have received an inheritance [a destiny – we were claimed by God as His own], having been predestined (chosen, appointed beforehand) according to the purpose of Him who works everything in agreement with the counsel and design of His will.'
Ephesians 1:11 AMP*

THE IDENTITY ISSUE

THE IDENTITY PROJECT

DAY 4:

A SOLID ROCK TO BUILD ON

> *'These words I speak to you are not incidental additions to your life, homeowner improvements to your standard of living. They are foundational words, words to build a life on.'*
> Matthew 7:24-25 MSG

I hope that by now you are starting to see that our identity, the way we see ourselves, forms the foundation upon which the rest of our lives are built. Let's consider this thought further.

I am sure you have seen a construction site before. I always find it exciting when large fences go up around a piece of vacant land or an old building. You know that something new and fresh is coming to that part of town. I am always surprised, though, at how much time passes before you can actually see anything start to happen. Sure, there are trucks and cranes and workmen around, but weeks, sometimes months, go by before any construction becomes visible. What are the crews working on during this time? Are they just sitting around refining the plans and working out where to start? Not at all. The work they are doing in those first few weeks might not look very impressive, but it is vital to the success of the whole project. They are building the foundation!

Foundations are important for two reasons. First of all, they determine how big the building that follows can become. The larger the building, the deeper the foundation needs to be. Secondly, they determine how long the building will stand. The stronger the foundation, the longer the building will remain intact, standing strong and secure despite shifts in the Earth around it.

Let's apply this concept to our own lives. If you picture your ultimate life as some kind of physical structure, what does it look like? I don't know about you, but I want to build a life that is large and long standing. I want there to be room in the world I build around myself for people to rest, feel loved, and be empowered to grow. And I want to be here for the long haul! I don't want anything falling apart, shifting or cracking when challenging times come along. What do I need to build this kind of life? You guessed it: a strong, solid foundation.

Jesus thinks that foundations are pretty important too! So important, in fact, that He mentioned them when He was here on Earth. What He said was recorded in the book of Matthew for us to continue to learn from today:

> *'These words I speak to you are not incidental additions to your life, homeowner improvements to your standard of living. They are foundational words, words to build a life on. If you work these words into your life, you are like a smart carpenter who built his house on solid rock. Rain poured down, the river flooded, a tornado hit—but nothing moved that house. It was*

> *fixed to the rock. But if you just use my words in Bible studies and don't work them into your life, you are like a stupid carpenter who built his house on the sandy beach. When a storm rolled in and the waves came up, it collapsed like a house of cards.'*
> Matthew 7:24-27 MSG

What a vivid picture this passage creates! When I read it, I can imagine in my mind two houses on a coastline. One is built into a rocky cliff and its foundations are sunk deep into the solid rock. Regardless of how wild the storms get, this house isn't going anywhere. The other house I see is build on the sand. It might look impressive and have amazing views, but when the winds blow and the rain comes, there is nothing holding it in place.

Now, when it comes to building our lives, I know which house I want my life to look like! And I don't think you would find many people out there who are hoping their lives collapse like a house of cards! So the question must be asked: how do we build a life on solid rock? Jesus said that the strongest foundation to build on was His Word. However, not just reading it, but working it into our daily lives, allowing it to deeply change and impact the way we live.

If our identity, the way we see ourselves, forms the foundation from which we view the world, make decisions and process the things that happen around us, then we must choose to build this foundation as strongly as possibly. It must be built on the truth of the Word of God.

PAUSE, PONDER, REFLECT

Questions to Reflect on:
Take stock of the foundations of your life right now. Are they solid? Are they shaky? Are cracks starting to appear? Have you built your identity on the truths of God's word and what He says about who you are?

Scriptures to ponder:
'Everyone who hears my teaching and applies it to his life can be compared to a wise man who built his house on an unshakable foundation. When the rains fell and the flood came, with fierce winds beating upon his house, it stood firm because of its strong foundation.'
Matthew 7:24-25 TPT

*'I will proclaim the name of the Lord.
Oh, praise the greatness of our God!
He is the Rock, His works are perfect,
and all His ways are just.
A faithful God who does no wrong,
upright and just is He.'*
Deuteronomy 32:3-4 NIV

'For the word of God is living and active and full of power [making it operative, energizing, and effective]. It is sharper than any two-edged sword, penetrating as far as the division of the soul and spirit [the completeness of a person], and of both joints and marrow [the deepest parts of our nature], exposing and judging the very thoughts and intentions of the heart.'
Hebrews 4:12 AMP

THE IDENTITY PROJECT

A SOLID ROCK TO BUILD ON

PART ONE

Marked

by the

Marker

- YOUR IDENTITY AS A PERSON CREATED IN THE IMAGE OF GOD -

DAY 5:

GOD DOESN'T MAKE MISTAKES

*'Then God said, "Let Us make man in Our
image, according to Our likeness".'
Genesis 1:26 NKJV*

As we start to unpack this important concept of identity and hopefully reshape and rebuild areas of your identity that have been warped or twisted, we are going to base everything on the truth of the Bible – God's Word. As we discovered yesterday, it is the strongest foundation on which to build our lives.

And in order to build a solid and enduring foundation, we are also going to go deep – four layers deep. As we move through these layers, they will become more and more personal and individual to *your* life and *your* unique identity. Before we begin to build this foundation, I thought it would be fitting to go all the way back to the very beginning, to the Garden of Eden.

You see, a huge aspect of our identity is found in the fact that we have been created by God. You are not an accident, a mistake, or the result of hundreds of millions of years and billions of evolutionary genetic mutations. You were created.

You were designed. You were hand made! Have you been to the markets lately or jumped on Etsy? Handmade stuff is expensive! Handmade things are special because of the time, care and effort that is involved in producing them. They aren't merely products off a production line. They have value because they are unique. Guess what? So do you. You have incredible value because you have been created by God.

Now that truth alone is powerful, but there is more. It gets better! Not only were you deliberately and intentionally created by God; you were also created in *His image*. Let's take another look at where this is mentioned in the book of Genesis:

'Then God said, "Let us make mankind in our image, in our likeness, so that they may rule over the fish in the sea and the birds in the sky, over the livestock and all the wild animals, and over all the creatures that move along the ground." So God created mankind in His own image, in the image of God He created them; male and female He created them.'
Genesis 1:26-27 NKJV

When the Bible says that we are made in God's image, it is saying that we are *like him!* It isn't saying that you are a god (sorry to burst that bubble), but you are *like* Him. You are a *representation;* you *share similar characteristics* to Him. In the same way that an artist pours himself into a painting and then finishes it by leaving his signature, you have been imprinted, marked and sealed by your maker. Your creator just also happens to be the Almighty God!

The fact that God created us gives *all* people incredible value. The fact that He created us *in His image* only increases this value. We live in a society that judges value based on appearance, ability, talent and material worth. However, your true value is based on far more than this. You have been created by God Himself!

Worth and value are also measured and determined by the price someone is willing to pay for something. Consider an auction, for example. The value of a piece of fine jewellery, an original painting or a beautiful property is ultimately determined by the price someone is willing to pay for it. Often at an auction, the predetermined value of an item will be superseded by the price a bidder is willing to pay to win the piece. When you consider your own value from this perspective, you are truly priceless. God paid the ultimate price to redeem you. He purchased you with the blood of His Son, Jesus. We will unpack this more in the second section of this journal, but for now, be reassured that your life has great worth and value and this value has been determined already by the One who created you in His image, and the incredible price He paid to redeem you.

If you were to ask God about your value today, He would whisper back to you: *'You are special because I made you, and I don't make mistakes. You have value because I paid the ultimate price to redeem you.'* The first stage in building a strong and true identity is understanding that you have value simply because you have been created in the image of God. We will discover what this means in detail over the next week.

PAUSE, PONDER, REFLECT

Questions to Reflect on:
How do you feel when you consider the truth that you have not only been hand made by God, but also made in His image? Does this change the way you view your self? How do you feel when you consider your value in light of the cross?

Scriptures to Ponder:

For you created my inmost being;
you knit me together in my mother's womb.
I praise you because I am fearfully and wonderfully made;
your works are wonderful,
I know that full well.
My frame was not hidden from you
when I was made in the secret place,
when I was woven together in the depths of the earth.
Your eyes saw my unformed body;
all the days ordained for me were written in your book
before one of them came to be.
How precious to me are your thoughts,[a] God!
How vast is the sum of them!
Were I to count them,
they would outnumber the grains of sand—
when I awake, I am still with you.'
Psalm 139:13-18 NIV

'Look at all the birds—do you think they worry about their existence? They don't plant or reap or store up food, yet your heavenly Father provides them each with food. Aren't you much more valuable to your Father than they? So, which one of you by worrying could add anything to your life?'
Matthew 6:26-27 TPT

GOD DOESN'T MAKE MISTAKES

THE IDENTITY PROJECT

DAY 6:
THE SEVEN MARKS OF THE MAKER

'I will praise You, for I am fearfully and wonderfully made.'
Psalm 139:14 NIV

As we have already discussed, you have been created in the image and likeness of God. This is incredible and gives you incredible value. But what does this statement really mean? In what ways do you actually reflect or represent God's likeness? This is a great question to ask and a great concept to explore.

In our quest to build a strong and solid sense of value and identity around our lives, we will unpack this together. It will become the first layer of our foundation, built on the truth of what the Word of God says about us.

Over the next seven days we will look at seven ways that we, as people created in the image of God, reflect His image.[1] All people, regardless of race, culture, gender or whether they have found the saving grace of Jesus or not, reflect the image of God in these seven ways. As we mentioned earlier, all people are created in the image of God and therefore all have value. You may be thinking, 'Well, if everyone shares this value, is it really value? How is my identity unique if I am created in God's image, along with every other person who has ever walked the planet?'

Your identity as someone created in the image of God is important because it sets the stage for everything else. As promised, we are going to dig down deep into your unique and personal identity as we move through this journal, however, it is important that we start here. The understanding of how we have been made in the image of God provides the foundation on which everything else will be built, so stick with me!

I like to think of these characteristics as imprints or markers. In the same way that envelopes used to be sealed with wax and stamped with the seal of the sender, we have been stamped and carry the seal of our creator. Each of these seven marks are characteristics that are unique to humanity, to those made in the image of God. They are the ways that we reflect His image and His likeness and they set us apart from all other aspects of creation. You may notice as you read through this list that you don't have to look very hard to see these characteristics in your own life, it is beautiful to see that we reflect our creator simply by being who He created us to be.

Seven Marks of the Maker
1. We are spiritual, as God is spirit
2. We are creative, as God is creative
3. We are intelligent, as God is intelligent

4. We communicate, as God communicates
5. We have the ability to relate to others, as God is relational
6. We have a moral compass, as God is right and holy
7. We have a sense of purpose, as God is purposeful in all He does

This list might seem like a lot to get your head around. Don't worry! We are going to look at each of these seven characteristics in more detail over the next few days, but I hope you are beginning to get excited about the extent to which God has poured Himself into you as His creation.

PAUSE, PONDER, REFLECT

Questions to Reflect on:
When you read the list of marks we carry of God our maker, what jumps out at you first? Why do you think this is? How do these characteristics add value to what you think it means to be made in God's image?

Scriptures to Ponder:
> 'Then God said, "Let us make mankind in our image, in our likeness, so that they may rule over the fish in the sea and the birds in the sky, over the livestock and all the wild animals, and over all the creatures that move along the ground." So God created mankind in His own image, in the image of God He created them; male and female He created them.'
> Genesis 1:26-27 NIV

'Now the Lord is the Spirit, and where the Spirit of the Lord is, there is freedom. And we all, who with unveiled faces contemplate the Lord's glory, are being transformed into His image with ever-increasing glory, which comes from the Lord, who is the Spirit.'
2 Corinthians 3:17-18 TPT

THE SEVEN MARKS OF THE MAKER

THE IDENTITY PROJECT

DAY 7:
YOU ARE A SPIRITUAL BEING

'God is sheer being itself - Spirit. Those who worship him must do it out of their very being, their spirits, their true selves, in adoration.'
John 4:24 MSG

If you had to describe God to someone, what would you say? Regardless of how much time and preparation you put into your answer, chances are that one of the first things that would come to mind would be that He is a Spirit. God is eternal and He is not constricted by a physical body. He lives outside the dimensions of space and time that control our lives. You could say that being a spirit is one of the *defining* characteristics of God. It sets Him apart like few other descriptions can. He is a spirit.

How amazing is it then to consider that the first imprint of God's image and likeness on us, as His creation, is our spirituality. When He chose to create us in His image, the first thing He chose to mark us with was this defining characteristic. Just as God is a spirit, He has made us spiritual beings too. You have a soul and you live in a body, but you *are* a spirit. In fact, your spirit is the truest part of you. It is the part of you that connects with God and it is the part of you that will live forever.

This innate, in-built desire for spirituality and spiritual connection that God has placed in each one of us is evidenced by the number of different religions that can be found on the planet today, not to mention the individual quests for truth or spirituality that many embark on. There is a need in each of our hearts to connect spiritually to someone greater than ourselves. It is a desire that was placed in each of our hearts by God and is one of the ways we reflect Him as beings created in His image.

Although unseen, your spirit is just as real as your physical body. Your spirit also has needs. Just as your body needs food, water, oxygen and sleep in order to function well, your spirit was designed to connect and engage in an intimate relationship with God. Without this, your spirit will starve. When we find and connect with God through Jesus, our spirit comes alive and begins to thrive and grow. When we receive the Holy Spirit our spirit is empowered and strengthened even further. The life our spirit receives as a result of intimacy with God permeates into every other area of our lives. It is only when our spirit is alive that we begin to feel truly alive and it is only when our spirit connects with the Spirit of God that true life and value begins to flood our identity and influence the way we see ourselves.

I can't think of a better way to begin building the first layer of true identity in our lives than by inviting the one who created us to connect with us on this journey. In the book of Revelation, Jesus paints a beautiful picture of the way He approaches our hearts:

> *'Behold, I stand at the door and knock. If anyone hears My voice and opens the door, I will come in to him and dine with him, and he with Me.'*
> Revelation 3:20

I love that Jesus doesn't force Himself into our lives. He knocks and leaves the response up to us. By going to the cross, He has done everything required to open the way for us, as broken spiritual beings, to connect with Him and be fully restored in our spiritual lives, but He waits to be invited. Today, will you open the door of your heart to Him?

Perhaps you already have a close walk with Jesus, but want to surrender all areas of your heart to Him again. Perhaps you have neglected your spiritual life for some time and need to reconnect with God, who loves you deeply. Or perhaps you have never prayed a prayer like this before. Perhaps today, for the first time in your life, you want to connect as a spiritual being to the Spirit who created you and loves you. You can pray the prayer written below if you like, or in your own words, simply invite Jesus into your heart and life. Be real, be honest and be open.

'Jesus, I invite you into my heart today. I recognise that I need you. On my own I have hurt myself, hurt others and hurt you through my words and actions. I have lived life on my own and I don't want to do this anymore. Thank you for dying on the cross to open the way for me to come back to you. Please forgive me of my sins and help me to build my life based on your truth. Please fill me now with your Holy Spirit and empower me to live the life you have planned for me. I surrender every part of my life to you. Please lead me and teach me how to live in relationship with you. Amen.'

PAUSE, PONDER, REFLECT

Questions to reflect on:
Have you ever considered that your spirit is the truest part of you? How does this perspective change the way you view your relationship with God? How well are you currently feeding and nurturing your spirit? What could you do today to connect with God today in a new or fresh way?

Scriptures to Ponder:
'But a time is coming and is already here when the true worshipers will worship the Father in spirit [from the heart, the inner self] and in truth; for the Father seeks such people to be His worshipers. God is spirit [the Source of life, yet invisible to mankind], and those who worship Him must worship in spirit and truth.'
John 4:23-24 AMP

'Then you will call on me and come and pray to me, and I will listen to you. You will seek me and find me when you seek me with all your heart.'
Jeremiah 29:12-13 NIV

YOU ARE A SPIRITUAL BEING

'So here's what I want you to do, God helping you: Take your everyday, ordinary life—your sleeping, eating, going-to-work, and walking-around life—and place it before God as an offering. Embracing what God does for you is the best thing you can do for him. Don't become so well-adjusted to your culture that you fit into it without even thinking. Instead, fix your attention on God. You'll be changed from the inside out.'
Romans 12:1 MSG

THE IDENTITY PROJECT

YOU ARE A SPIRITUAL BEING

DAY 8:

YOU ARE CREATIVE

*'The heavens declare the glory of God; the
skies proclaim the work of his Hands.
Day after day they pour forth speech; night
after night they reveal knowledge.'*
Psalm 19:1-2 NIV

God is creative. Undeniably creative. Extraordinarily creative! The creation account found in Genesis tells us this, as does creation itself! You only need to take a look around you to hear it calling forth the beauty and wonder of a truly creative God. Consider the majestic mountain ridges, the deep ocean reefs and the far-flung galaxies. Ponder the diversity we see between glaciers and deserts, mountain tops and valleys, and we haven't even begun to consider the creativity displayed in the animals found on this wild and wondrous planet. God is incredibly creative and as His creation made in His image. You are too!

Your creative ability is one of the ways you reflect the image of God. It is another stamp, another marker, that God the creator has imprinted on us as His creation. Now, before you try to tell me that you aren't creative, I want to stop you. You are!

I think that, in many ways, we have incorrectly limited our understanding of creativity to the arts. Now, please, don't misunderstand me here, I love the arts. However, often when people hear the word creativity they think of paintings, music, dance, drama and nothing more. And while art is incredibly important and valuable, the truth is that creativity is so much more than just these expressions. Creativity is involved in all kinds of design: creating systems, lateral thinking, working with others well and finding solutions to complex problems. Creativity is a vital part of life! In every field, whether it be medicine, technology, science, education, design, politics and more, major breakthroughs have always been preceded by creative thinking. New ideas are born when people are brave enough to think outside the box, search for new ways of doing things and explore new possibilities. These are all expressions of true creativity.

Creativity also finds its place in our everyday lives – from cooking, to maintaining schedules, to finding new ways to get your children to eat their veggies. Regardless of whether you sing or dance or believe you are a creative person, the truth is that every single one of us is creative because we are made in the image of a creative God. Every time creativity is expressed in our lives, it reflects the most creative one of all: our creator.

What a beautiful stone this is to lay in the foundation we are building together. As someone created in the image of God, you are creative!

What value and worth this truth brings to your identity. You have the ability to bring forth life, to create things that are not yet here, to dream about the new and bring it into the present. You, my friend, are inherently creative. Do not ever fall into the trap of believing the lie that you are not, or the lie that you do not have anything valuable to contribute to your world. You do and you can. It is who you are!

PAUSE, PONDER, REFLECT

Questions to Reflect on:
What would your life look like if you lived every day believing with all your heart that you were truly creative? What would it look like if you believed that within you, placed there by God, was the ability to bring forth life, to create new things, to explore unknown possibilities and to express love creatively? What dreams would you pursue if you truly embraced this perspective of truth?

Scriptures to Ponder:
'In the beginning was the Word, and the Word was with God, and the Word was God. He was with God in the beginning. Through Him all things were made; without Him nothing was made that has been made. In Him was life, and that life was the light of all mankind. The light shines in the darkness, and the darkness has not overcome it.'
John 1:1-5 NIV

*'But ask the animals, and they will teach you,
or the birds in the sky, and they will tell you;
or speak to the earth, and it will teach you,
or let the fish in the sea inform you.
Which of all these does not know
that the hand of the Lord has done this?
In his hand is the life of every creature
and the breath of all mankind.'
Job 12:7-10 NIV*

*'For since the creation of the world God's invisible qualities—His eternal power and divine nature—have been clearly seen, being understood from what has been made, so that people are without excuse.'
Romans 1:20 NIV*

YOU ARE CREATIVE

DAY 9:

YOU ARE INTELLIGENT

*'What a miracle of skin and bone, muscle and brain!
You gave me life itself, and incredible love. You
watched and guarded every breath I took.'*
Job 10:11-12 MSG

Welcome to Day 9! I hope and pray that God has been revealing new truth to you about the way you have been created over the last few days. Now, if you have found yourself on this journey of identity discovery because you feel your self-image doesn't paint an accurate picture of who you are, you might find yourself balking at some of the truths we are unpacking in these pages. Yesterday we considered how innately creative you are and we will look at how incredibly intelligent you are today. Please know that it is completely okay if these discussions bring up mixed emotions, painful memories, or past hurt in your heart. That is absolutely what this journey is all about and why there is so much space included in this journal to write everyday. If you have built your identity on the shifting sand of what others have said about you, unrealistic expectations or false beliefs, chances are that there will be many things that need to be pulled up in your heart and replaced with truth.

YOU ARE INTELLIGENT

Begin to think of your heart as a garden. With the help of the Holy Spirit, you are coming each day and asking Him to identify weeds that need to be uprooted and replaced with seeds that will grow into life giving blooms. You might feel a little bit uncomfortable with this thought, but be reassured that the Holy Spirit is an excellent gardener and an expert in turning thorny broken beds of weeds into thriving gardens of living colour!

So, let's get right into it. Today we will be focusing on how intelligent you are. Don't get carried away with old ways of thinking that are not founded on truth when you read these sentences. I want to declare over you today that you are intelligent. Incredibly intelligent!

It doesn't matter what people have said in the past about how smart you are, or what you have come to believe about your abilities in this area. It doesn't even really matter how well you scored in school exams. The truth is that you are intelligent because you are made in the image of an intelligent God. Consider your brain for a moment, the most complex and intricately designed computer system the world will ever know! Even as you sit and read these words, millions of electrical impulses are connecting. They are forming thoughts and building memories, recalling existing information and evaluating this new information against it. And all of this is happening right now, without you even thinking about it! Please don't try to tell me you are not intelligent. You are incredibly intelligent!

This is the third way that we reflect the image of God, our creator. It is another mark, or imprint, of His nature that He has chosen to pass on to us as people made in His image. God is full of wisdom and knowledge and has created us with the ability to learn and understand. He has also given us the ability to think, to reason, to remember and to critically evaluate the information we receive.

Yes, some people may be more gifted in certain areas than others and we are definitely not all called to be rocket scientists or brain surgeons. But a core part of our identity as people created in the image of God is the fact that we are intelligent beings. And God has given you exactly what you need between your ears to fulfill the call and plan that He has for your life!

PAUSE, PONDER, REFLECT

Questions to Reflect on:
What you have come to believe about your intelligence? What influences have shaped this perspective? Are these beliefs founded in truth? How have these beliefs filtered into other areas of your heart and life? Do some of them need to change?

Often careless or thoughtless words spoken over us can leave deep and lasting wounds in our hearts. Do you need to speak with a trusted friend or mentor about the way you feel when you answer these questions? It may be painful to unravel the emotions around such wounds. Ask God to show you the people in your world that can help you bring truth to this important area of your identity.

Scriptures to Ponder:

'Brothers and sisters, think of what you were when you were called. Not many of you were wise by human standards; not many were influential; not many were of noble birth. But God chose the foolish things of the world to shame the wise; God chose the weak things of the world to shame the strong.'
1 Corinthians 1:26-27 NIV

He answered, 'Love the Lord your God with all your heart and with all your soul and with all your strength and with all your mind'; and, 'Love your neighbour as yourself.'
John 10:27 NIV

'I praise you because I am fearfully and wonderfully made;
your works are wonderful,
I know that full well.
My frame was not hidden from you
when I was made in the secret place,
when I was woven together in the depths of the earth.
Your eyes saw my unformed body;
all the days ordained for me were written in your book
before one of them came to be.'
Psalm 139: 14-17 NIV

THE IDENTITY PROJECT

YOU ARE INTELLIGENT

DAY 10:

YOU COMMUNICATE

*'Then God said, "Let there be light"; and there was light.
And God saw the light, that it was good.'*
Genesis 1:3-4 NIV

Our God is a speaking God, and when He speaks, things happen! His words are powerful and His words bring life. In Genesis, we read that God used words to create the world. He spoke everything we see into existence. Talk about words that hold power.

How incredible is it, then, to consider that God speaks to us; that He takes the time to look into our lives and direct His powerful voice into our hearts? In the book of Zephaniah, it is recorded that God even sings over us, that He quiets us with His love. When I read that verse, the image that always comes to mind is of a mother singing a lullaby over her child. That's how God feels about you. Talk about special!

But we are not focusing today on the fact that God speaks. We are going to consider how powerful it is that He has gifted *us* with the ability to speak. As human beings, created in the image of God, we have been given the ability to communicate, the ability to use words. When you consider the rest of creation, there is no other creature that has been given this privilege. Sure, animals use sounds and noises to communicate with each other, sometimes in very sophisticated ways. However, an animal's ability to communicate is incredibly limited compared to our ability as humans. Have you ever seen two rabbits have an in-depth, two-hour long conversation about their relationships? Maybe in a Disney movie!

Our ability to speak and communicate is actually another one of the ways that we reflect the image of God our creator. It is another way we carry the mark of our maker in the very core of who we are.

And, just as God's words are powerful, your words are powerful too.

We use words everyday, often without a second thought as to the power they hold. Words tell stories and give compliments. They tell jokes, sing songs, order coffee, ask questions, encourage others and give directions. Words, however, also have a dark side. They can gossip, they can lie, they can be used to criticise, or to pull others down. There are few things in life that are as painful as the sting of a harsh word. The regret that comes from realising that you have hurt people you love with careless conversation can remain with you long after the words have left your lips. The regret of words left unsaid can also haunt our hearts. I am sure that every single one of us has experienced the power that words hold – both for good and for evil.

It is so important that we use this incredible gift well and be sure to use our words wisely, but today, I want you to firstly consider how valued you must be to God to have been entrusted with this powerful privilege in the first place. What a gift that He has placed in each of our lives by giving us this ability to communicate.

Can you see the picture that we are slowly building here of your identity as a person who has been handmade in the image of God? Firstly, you are a spiritual being who is also creative and highly intelligent, and you have also been given the powerful gift of communication. What value and worth your life holds in considering these aspects of your identity alone – but we are only half way there!

PAUSE, PONDER, REFLECT

Questions to Reflect on:
Your ability to communicate is one of the ways you reflect the image of God, who created the world with words. How does this thought change the way you think about your words and how you use them? Think about the way words have shaped you and influenced your life. Can you see the power they hold? Evaluate the words you have spoken recently to people close to you. Are your words gentle, nurturing and encouraging? Does anything need to be adjusted? What about the way you speak about yourself? How can you make your words life giving today?

Scriptures to Ponder:

'Your God is present among you,
a strong Warrior there to save you.
Happy to have you back, He'll calm you with his love
and delight you with his songs.'
Zephaniah 3:17 MSG

'Let your conversation be always full of grace, seasoned with salt, so that you may know how to answer everyone.'
Colossians 4:6

'Do not let any unwholesome talk come out of your mouths, but only what is helpful for building others up according to their needs, that it may benefit those who listen.'
Ephesians 4:29

'We all stumble in many ways. Anyone who is never at fault in what they say is perfect, able to keep their whole body in check. When we put bits into the mouths of horses to make them obey us, we can turn the whole animal. Or take ships as an example. Although they are so large and are driven by strong winds, they are steered by a very small rudder wherever the pilot wants to go. Likewise, the tongue is a small part of the body, but it makes great boasts. Consider what a great forest is set on fire by a small spark.'
James 3:2-5

THE IDENTITY PROJECT

YOU COMMUNICATE

DAY 11:

YOU ARE RELATIONAL

*'The Lord God said, "It is not good for the man
to be alone. I will make a helper,
a companion suitable for him."'*
Genesis 2:18 NIV

Our God is a relational God. He is one God in three persons – the Father, The Son and the Holy Spirit. Our God exists continually and eternally in vibrant, perfect relationship within this Trinity. And guess what? When He created you in His image, He designed you with the ability to engage in intimate and meaningful relationships too. This is the fifth way that we reflect the image of our Creator.

First and foremost, God designed you to live in relationship with Him; to walk each day connected intimately to your Creator. Remember how we discussed your spirituality as the first way you reflect the image of God? These two markers were designed to work hand in hand together. In Genesis, we read that Adam walked with God in Eden. He experienced a deep, personal and meaningful relationship with his Creator. Although sin later separated Adam (and all who would follow) from this perfect relationship, the desire of the Father has always been to bring us back to 'the garden' and to restore us to this place of intimate connection that we were created for. Through Jesus, this has been accomplished and the way has been opened once again for each of us to enter into a meaningful, personal relationship with God. A relationship you were designed and created to engage in with all of your spirit, soul and body – a relationship like no other.

Secondly, God has given you the ability to connect relationally so that you can live in relationship with others. And just think for a moment how boring life would be if we didn't! After God created Adam in Genesis chapter 2, He declared that it was 'not good for Him to be alone' (Genesis 2:18). This is actually the first thing we find in the scriptures that is 'not good'. Throughout the creation account, God declared that everything was good, until he realised that man was alone. The sun and the moon were declared as good, the oceans and the sky were declared as good. All of the creatures of the land and sea and air were declared as good. However, God realised that it was

> *not good for Adam to be alone. It was after this that He created Eve, the perfect helper and companion for Adam.*

How refreshing is it to think that relationships, families and communities were all God's idea! He created us to enjoy them and be enriched by them. We have been wired for connection, created for intimacy and designed for relationships. These needs and desires are planted deeply within you and are another one of the ways you carry the mark of your creator – the relational God.

Finally, when considering the depths of our personal relationships today, how beautiful is it to consider that when revealing Himself to us, God chose to do so out of relationship? He could have chosen to reveal Himself to us primarily as a King, which He is, and placed us in the picture as His servants, but He doesn't. He could have chosen to reveal Himself to us as a judge, which He is, and placed us in the picture as His subjects, but He doesn't. Instead, He chooses primarily to reveal Himself in the scriptures as a *Father* and invites us to participate in His story as His *children*. What a beautiful image of the relationship He desires us to have with us and has empowered us to have with Him.

PAUSE, PONDER, REFLECT

Questions to Reflect on:
Have you ever considered your ability to relate to others as a gift from God or as part of the way that you reflect His image? How does this thought add value to who you are and how does it shape your identity? Take a moment to reflect on your relationship with God. Do you connect or speak with Him like you would a close friend or family member? Do you think He desires this kind of relationship with you?

Scriptures to Ponder:
'Jesus answered him, "'Love the Lord your God with every passion of your heart, with all the energy of your being, and with every thought that is within you.' This is the great and supreme commandment. And the second is like it in importance: 'You must love your friend in the

same way you love yourself.' Contained within these commandments to love you will find all the meaning of the Law and the Prophets."'
Matthew 22:37-40 TPT

'Here I am! I stand at the door and knock. If anyone hears my voice and opens the door, I will come in and eat with that person, and they with me.'
Revelation 3:20 NIV

'Dear friends, let us love one another, for love comes from God. Everyone who loves has been born of God and knows God. Whoever does not love does not know God, because God is love.'
1 John 4:7-8 NIV

THE IDENTITY PROJECT

YOU ARE RELATIONAL

DAY 12:

YOU HAVE A MORAL COMPASS

'And you shall know the truth, and the truth shall make you free.' John 8:32

Have you ever wondered where your conscience came from? You know, that little sting you feel inside when you make a choice that hurts someone close to you? Maybe you say something without thinking, or make a silly mistake… and ouch! There it is, quietly letting you know inside that something has gone wrong, or that a relationship will need to be repaired in some way.

Today, I want to consider the truth that each of us has been given an internal compass designed to pull us towards right action and right living. Your conscience. It is actually another one of the ways in which you have been marked by the one who made you in His likeness, a gift given to you by your Creator to help guide you morally.

The more I think about this, the more I am amazed at how intricately God has designed and created each one of us. God is pure, He is holy and He is everything just and true. He is light and in Him is no darkness. How wonderfully kind is it that He has placed within us a moral compass to pull us towards Himself; a compass to pull us towards thoughts and actions that are pure, and to pull us towards justice, truth and light. This internal compass reminds us that we have moral responsibility – we have been created to act in ways that are beneficial to others and ourselves, rather than making choices that cause harm. Any time you feel a desire for truth, justice or righteousness, it is a reminder of the true, just and righteous God who made you in His image. This is the sixth way we reflect the image of our Creator.

American journalist H.L. Menchken once wrote that 'Conscience is the inner voice that warns us somebody may be looking.' Isn't that the truth! Every decision we make, every word we speak, even every thought that enters our minds – weather in public or behind closed doors – is seen by someone – your Father in Heaven. Nothing goes unnoticed. Nothing is hidden from Him. This thought can be incredibly confronting or incredibly comforting, depending on how you view the one who is watching over you. My hope and prayer is that you would come to know and understand God as a loving, gracious and compassionate father, one who loves you so much, that He has put within you a moral compass to pull you towards Himself.

So how does this internal moral compass contribute to our identity? How does this add to our value and worth as people created in the image of God? Simply by reminding us who we are and who we belong to. Every time our conscience is engaged or activated, it should remind us of the one who placed it there, pointing us continually back to the loving, kind Father who created us and desires us to live a life of purpose and significance as His children.

PAUSE, PONDER, REFLECT

Questions to Reflect on:
Have you previously thought about your conscience and where it might have come from? How does the knowledge that God has placed it within you change your perspective? How does it empower you to live a life that is strong and clean? How do you feel it adds to your value and sense of worth? Allow your conscience to be your guard when using social media and navigating the online world driven by opinion. Check your spirit before you hit 'post' on that photo, comment or share.

Scriptures to Ponder:
> *'He has made everything beautiful in its time. He has also set eternity in the human heart; yet no one can fathom what God has done from beginning to end.'*
> *Ecclesiastes 3:11 NIV*

> *'Whether you turn to the right or to the left, your ears will hear a voice behind you, saying, "This is the way; walk in it." '*
> *Isaiah 30:21 NIV*

YOU HAVE A MORAL COMPASS

'They show that the essential requirements of the Law are written in their hearts; and their conscience [their sense of right and wrong, their moral choices] bearing witness and their thoughts alternately accusing or perhaps defending them.'
Romans 2:15 AMP

THE IDENTITY PROJECT

YOU HAVE A MORAL COMPASS

DAY 13:

YOU HAVE A SENSE OF PURPOSE

'"For I know the plans I have for you," declares the Lord, "plans to prosper you and not to harm you, plans to give you hope and a future".'
Jeremiah 29:11 NIV

Today we lay the final stone in this first foundation of our identity as people created in the image of God. You were created *on purpose* and *for a great purpose*. What powerful thoughts to consider.

Regardless of what may have been spoken over you, or what you may feel about your life, the truth is that there are no mistakes, no accidents and no coincidences when it comes to God's plan for you and His purposes for your life. He does things on purpose, with purpose and you are no different.

Do not let anyone fool you into thinking, even for a minute, that you have been placed on Earth by chance. No. You, my friend, are here on purpose, to fill a role that only you can. And not only that, God has created you with a great sense of purpose built into your spirit. There are important and significant things that you are here to do!

YOU HAVE A SENSE OF PURPOSE

Living with purpose could be described as the desire to become and accomplish all that you can during this lifetime, to contribute to the world in a meaningful way and to leave behind something larger or more significant than yourself. What this looks like for you personally is something that only you can uncover, although it is my prayer that this journal helps you take a few steps in that direction.

Purpose for you may be found in family. It may be in raising healthy, strong passionate and secure children, or in building a marriage that shines as an example of selfless and faithful love.

Purpose for you may be found in business. For you to create and promote ideas that contribute meaningfully to our world and in watching them grow and flourish.

Purpose for you may be found in giving. That is, in using the gifts and abilities you have to serve humanity at its point of greatest need.

Purpose for you could be in sharing your knowledge with others. This could be by helping people navigate the challenges of life or by opening your home to be a place of safety and connection.

Your purpose may be a combination of many of these things, or something else entirely. But be sure to know that the greatest joy and fulfillment you will find in life will be in discovering and accomplishing the purpose God has placed in your heart.

In the book of Esther, the Bible tells a beautiful story of discovering purpose, and the risk often required to step into your destiny. When we first meet Esther, she is a young, orphaned Jewish girl living in a Persian occupied land with her uncle. Through an unusual turn of events, she finds herself becoming queen, just as a political plan to annihilate all of her people is put into action. When speaking to her Uncle about what she should do in light of the situation, he points her towards her purpose and destiny by saying, 'who knows, but that you have been bought to this position for such a time as this.' (Esther 4:14). Risking her life, Esther chooses to speak up for her people and, as a result of her bravery, is able to save them.

Just as Queen Esther discovered, I believe that each one of us has been born 'for such a time as this'. How amazing that God wants to partner with us in achieving His plans on the Earth! There is a measure of personal responsibility, however, that must be considered when we look at purpose. Esther had to choose and prepare to walk in purpose. If she had chosen to remain silent, God would have brought help and deliverance to His people from another place, but Esther would have missed the great adventure placed before her by God.

To recognise and understand that your life has purpose is the seventh way that we reflect God's image. The in-built desire to live with purpose and meaning is a gift from God, and to live each day with a sense of purpose is the seventh seal, stamp, or mark that the Maker leaves on us as His creation. What worth and value this adds to our lives! Choose to take a step forward in discovering or walking in your purpose today!

PAUSE, PONDER, REFLECT

Questions to Reflect on:
You were designed on purpose and for a great purpose, by a God who loves you. Have you ever considered this before? How does it make you feel? How does it change the way you see yourself and your life? What feelings of hope and expectancy are stirred in your heart when you ponder this truth?

Scriptures to Ponder:
'He has made everything beautiful and appropriate in its time. He has also planted eternity [a sense of divine purpose] in the human heart [a mysterious longing which nothing under the sun can satisfy, except God]—yet man cannot find out (comprehend, grasp) what God has done (His overall plan) from the beginning to the end.'
Ecclesiastes 3:11 AMP

'And we know [with great confidence] that God [who is deeply concerned about us] causes all things to work together [as a plan] for good for those who love God, to those who are called according to His plan and purpose.'
Romans 8:28 AMP

'You are not forgotten, for you have been chosen and destined by Father God. The Holy Spirit has set you apart to be God's holy ones, obedient followers of Jesus Christ who have been gloriously sprinkled with his blood. May God's delightful grace and peace cascade over you many times over!'
1 Peter 1:2 TPT

YOU HAVE A SENSE OF PURPOSE

THE IDENTITY PROJECT

DAY 14:

FALLEN WITH THE CHANCE TO BE FULLY RESTORED

'And the God of all grace, who called you to His eternal glory in Christ, after you have suffered a little while, will Himself restore you and make you strong, firm and steadfast.'
1 Peter 5:10 NIV

Over the last two weeks, we have considered the value our lives hold, simply because God chose to make us in His own image and we have looked in detail at what this specifically means. We have discovered that our spirituality, our creativity, our intelligence, our ability to communicate and relate to others, our conscience and our sense of purpose are all different ways that we reflect, simply by being who we are, the loving God who created us.

Each of these aspects of our humanity contribute value and worth to our identity because they reveal the One who created us. They aren't actually dependent on our actions and our value does not increase or decrease depending on how well we feel we are doing in each area. They are simply the marks in our lives that point back to our Maker. Like hallmarks on a piece of fine jewelry, they reveal our worth and value, regardless of the condition we find our lives in.

Adam and Eve walked in the garden with God. They experienced the joy and beauty of a sinless world and perfect relationships until they ate the fruit God had commanded them not to. Today, we live in a world where the effects of sin and the fallen human nature have tried to scar every one of the seven markers of God's image on humanity. Our relationships struggle, our moral compasses waver and fail, our sense of purpose is distorted and our desire to connect spiritually can lead almost anywhere. Yet a solid gold ring does not loose its value just because it ends up dirty and tarnished. In the same way, your value and worth as a human being created in the image of God does not change based on how good your life may or may not look right now. No, you are inherently valuable because of the One who created you.

There is, however, opportunity for restoration and complete healing to occur in every area of our lives through Jesus. When He left Heaven to live as a man here on Earth and went to the cross as an innocent man, He provided a way back into perfect relationship with God. Through the amazing, unearned and undeserved grace that is available to us in Jesus, we can find every part of our lives redeemed and restored. Through salvation and redemption, we are given not only forgiveness of our sins and eternal life, but also the opportunity to become *fully human* again here on the Earth and to have every part of our humanity restored.

It is God's desire that you live everyday in the fullness of all that He created you to be: spiritually, physically, intellectually, relationally and emotionally, all wrapped up in a sense of great purpose. I don't know about you, but I think that is an awesome way to live!

If there are areas of your life that you believe are still broken and tarnished, place them before God and ask Him to restore them. He is the healer of the broken hearted and He loves to bind the wounds of His children (Psalm 147:3).

PAUSE, PONDER, REFLECT

Questions to Reflect on:
How do you feel when you consider the truth that you have been handmade, wonderfully and beautifully, in the image of an awesome God? Which of the seven marks of the Marker meant the most to you? Why? How does knowing and understanding your value as someone created in the image of God help to build a strong identity in your life?

Scripture to Ponder:
> 'For we are His workmanship [His own master work, a work of art], created in Christ Jesus [reborn from above—spiritually transformed, renewed, ready to be used] for good works, which God prepared [for us] beforehand [taking paths which He set], so that we would walk in them [living the good life which He prearranged and made ready for us].'
> Ephesians 2:10 AMP

'Instead of your [former] shame you will have a double portion; And instead of humiliation your people will shout for joy over their portion. Therefore in their land they will possess double [what they had forfeited]; Everlasting joy will be theirs.'
Isaiah 61:7 AMP

'So repent [change your inner self—your old way of thinking, regret past sins] and return [to God—seek His purpose for your life], so that your sins may be wiped away [blotted out, completely erased], so that times of refreshing may come from the presence of the Lord [restoring you like a cool wind on a hot day]; and that He may send [to you] Jesus, the Christ, who has been appointed for you, whom heaven must keep until the time for the [complete] restoration of all things about which God promised through the mouth of His holy prophets from ancient time.'
Acts 3:19-21 AMP

FALLEN WITH THE CHANCE TO BE FULLY RESTORED

THE IDENTITY PROJECT

FALLEN WITH THE CHANCE TO BE FULLY RESTORED

PART TWO

found

IN

family

— YOUR IDENTITY IN CHRIST —

DAY 15:

THE BORN AGAIN IDENTITY

'Therefore, if anyone is in Christ, he is a new creation; old things have passed away; behold, all things have become new.'
2 Corinthians 5:17 NKJV

During the first section of this journal, we have looked at what it truly means to be made in the image of God. This is the first and most universal aspect of our identity. All people have been created in the image of God and each of our lives holds incredible value simply because of this truth. If this was all there was to discover about who we are, it would be enough for us to build a solid and strong identity. But there is so much more!

In this section of our journey, we will add another layer to the foundation we have begun to build, digging deeper into the truth of who we are. We have already discussed the importance of strong foundations, but let me take a moment today to remind you of their significance. How tall a tree can grow is directly related to how deep its roots go. The height of a skyscraper is determined by how deep the foundations are laid. It is so important that your identity is built on a solid and firm foundation. Discovering your identity as a person created in the image of God is only the first layer of this foundation. The second layer is discovering your identity as a person redeemed by the cross and now alive in Christ and part of God's family.

The truth of who you are in Christ is so important to grasp. If you fail to realise the value and power of the cross, you will also fail to realise your value, because the cross was for you! Yes, the cross reveals our sin, it reveals our brokenness and the need that each of us has for a saviour. But have you ever considered that the cross also reveals our value? It cost the Father His own Son to redeem you – and He considered you worth it!

The title of today's devotion is inspired by the 2006 movie *'The Bourne Identity.'* You may have seen it (or one of its many sequels). In the film, Jason Bourne wakes up after a blow to the head with no idea who he is, but retains only fleeting, blurry memories of his life. He spends most of the movie, and the many that follow, trying to understand and discover his true identity. I believe that there are far too many Christians wandering around today just like Jason Borne, with no idea of their true identity in Christ, their *born again identity*. They haven't really understood or grasped the magnitude of what Jesus did for them when He went to the cross, and this keeps them from stepping into their full purpose in life. Maybe you feel a little like that yourself. Don't worry – over the next 10 days we are going to dig down deep together to explore this significant aspect of our identity and build a strong foundation around the truth of who God says we are.

Let's begin by looking at a key passage of scripture that reveals clearly who we are in Christ and allow it to form the basis of our study over the coming days.

> *'Praise be to the God and Father of our Lord Jesus Christ, who has blessed us in the heavenly realms with every spiritual blessing in Christ. For He chose us in Him before the creation of the world to be holy and blameless in his sight. In love He predestined us for adoption to sonship through Jesus Christ, in accordance with His pleasure and will – to the praise of his glorious grace, which He has freely given us in the One He loves. In him we have redemption through his blood, the forgiveness of sins, in accordance with the riches of God's grace that He lavished on us... In Him we were also chosen, having been predestined according to the plan of Him who works out everything in conformity with the purpose of His will... And you also were included in Christ when you heard the message of truth, the gospel of your salvation. When you believed, you were marked in Him with a seal, the promised Holy Spirit, who is a deposit guaranteeing our inheritance until the redemption of those who are God's possession – to the praise of his glory.'*
> Ephesians 1:3-14

There is so much in these verses. They are jam packed with words that describe and define who we are in Christ. Over the following pages we will look at some of the words listed here in more detail. They paint a vibrant and empowering picture of who you are in Christ.

PAUSE, PONDER, REFLECT

Questions to Reflect on:
When you read the scripture above, what words jump out at you? Think for a moment about the phrase 'born again'. Jesus used this phrase when speaking with Nicodemus, a man who came to Him seeking truth in the middle of the night. He told Nicodemus that anyone who wanted to see the Kingdom of God must be born again, or born of the Spirit. What do you think the term means in regard to your identity and the way you see yourself?

Scriptures to Ponder:
'Now there was a certain man among the Pharisees named Nicodemus, a ruler (member of the Sanhedrin) among the Jews, who came to Jesus at night and said to Him, "Rabbi (Teacher), we know [without any doubt] that You have come from God as a teacher; for no one can do these signs [these wonders, these attesting miracles] that You do unless God is with him." Jesus answered him, "I assure you and most solemnly say to you, unless a person is born again [reborn from above—spiritually transformed, renewed, sanctified], he cannot [ever] see and experience the kingdom of God." Nicodemus said to Him, "How can a man be born when he is old? He cannot enter his mother's womb a second time and be born, can he?" Jesus answered, "I assure you and most solemnly say to you, unless one is born of water and the Spirit he cannot [ever] enter the kingdom of God. That which is born of the flesh is flesh [the physical is merely physical], and that which is born of the Spirit

is spirit. Do not be surprised that I have told you, 'You must be born again [reborn from above – spiritually transformed, renewed, sanctified].' The wind blows where it wishes and you hear its sound, but you do not know where it is coming from and where it is going; so it is with everyone who is born of the Spirit."
John 3:1-8 AMP

'Now, if anyone is enfolded into Christ, he has become an entirely new creation. All that is related to the old order has vanished. Behold, everything is fresh and new.'
2 Corinthians 5:17 TPT

'He came to save us. Not because of any virtuous deed that we have done, but only because of His extravagant mercy.'
Titus 3:5

THE BORN AGAIN IDENTITY

THE IDENTITY PROJECT

DAY 16:

FOUND IN FAMILY

*'The whole of creation waits breathless with
anticipation for the revelation of
God's sons and daughters.'*
Romans 8:19 CEB

We are going to spend some time considering the importance of family today, as all of our discussions over the next week will be built on the truth that we have been welcomed into the family of God. Considering that each one of us has our own varied experiences when it comes to family, I feel it's important to take some time on this issue. Even the best families are made up of imperfect people and it is important that we allow the Holy Spirit to search our hearts in this area and reveal any misconceptions about family that we might not even realise we are carrying.

We see the image of family woven all throughout the scriptures. In fact, family was the first institution created by God right back in Genesis 2. He looked at Adam and Eve and decreed prophetically that a man would leave his father and mother to create a whole new family unit with his wife (Genesis 2:24). Family was God's idea and it was the *first* institution He put in place on the Earth. I believe that in His original, ideal plan for creation, God designed family to be the primary way in which His glory would be revealed on the Earth. He created family long before He created the church, and long before He gave people rules and laws to live by. Family is really important to Him.

In fact, family is so important to God that He chose to reveal Himself to us in terms that come from family. He is a Father, Jesus is the Son, and the Holy Spirit is a close and intimate friend. Through the cross we also become His *children.* Sons and daughters of God. How significant! I love that God chooses these relationships that we all identify with and have experienced in one way or another, to represent the relationship He longs to have with us.

The relationship between a father and his children speaks of so many things. It represents firstly safety, security and provision. A good father will ensure that His children have everything they need, and God is a good father. Safety, security and provision can all be found in personal relationship with Him. Secondly, this relationship speaks of deep connection. A good father knows His children well and loves them deeply, and God is a good father. He knows every detail of your life and loves you with an unconditional, overwhelming and everlasting love. Thirdly, this relationship speaks of responsibility and discipline. A good father loves His children enough to teach them how to become responsible men and women of Godly character, and again, God is a good father. His desire is that as we grow in our relationship with Him, we would also grow to become more like him. As we live in deep and personal relationship with Him, we find ourselves changing and adjusting the way we live, not as a response to rules, but out of connection and intimacy. Learning to live as a follower of Christ is really all about learning to live in family!

The truth is that everything we have in Jesus, including a solid and strong identity, comes from the fact that we have been welcomed into the family of God. We are not servants, we are not slaves, and we are not just followers. No, we are His sons and daughters. We are His children. We are called His friends.

PAUSE, PONDER, REFLECT

Questions to Reflect on:
What have your experiences been like with family so far in life? Have you transferred any of these beliefs or experiences to the way you see God and relate to Him as a father? Ask the Holy Spirit to highlight areas of your heart that need healing in this area. He is still in the business of restoring brokenness and making all things new. If you have been let down, pushed aside, or hurt by your earthly father, invite God into these areas of pain and ask Him to bring healing and wholeness to these areas of your life.

Scriptures to Ponder:
'Love is patient, love is kind. It does not envy, it does not boast, it is not proud. It does not dishonor others, it is not self-seeking, it is not easily angered, it keeps no record of wrongs. Love

does not delight in evil but rejoices with the truth. It always protects, always trusts, always hopes, always perseveres.'
1 Corinthians 13:4-7 NIV

'Follow God's example, therefore, as dearly loved children and walk in the way of love, just as Christ loved us and gave himself up for us as a fragrant offering and sacrifice to God.'
Ephesians 5:1-2 NIV

'See what an incredible quality of love the Father has shown to us, that we would [be permitted to] be named and called and counted the children of God! And so we are! For this reason the world does not know us, because it did not know Him. Beloved, we are [even here and] now children of God, and it is not yet made clear what we will be [after His coming]. We know that when He comes and is revealed, we will [as His children] be like Him, because we will see Him just as He is [in all His glory]. And everyone who has this hope [confidently placed] in Him purifies himself, just as He is pure (holy, undefiled, guiltless).'
1 John 3:1-3 AMP

DAY 17:
YOU WERE PREDESTINED

'Even as He chose us in Him before the foundation of the world, that we should be holy and blameless before Him. In love He predestined us for adoption as sons through Jesus Christ, according to the purpose of His will.'
Ephesians 1:4-5 ESV

The scriptures state that God *chose you*, in fact *predestined* you, to be found in His Son, Jesus, before the foundations of the world were laid. Stop and think about that for a moment! God knew you were coming and was really excited about it! In fact, He planned it and planned *for* it. In case you haven't worked it out yet, God likes you! He really, really likes you! I think that David, the shepherd boy who became a great King of Israel, was beginning to understand this when he wrote Psalm 139:

*My frame was not hidden from you
when I was made in the secret place,
when I was woven together in the depths of the earth.
Your eyes saw my unformed body;
all the days ordained for me were written in your book
before one of them came to be.
How precious to me are your thoughts, God!*

How vast is the sum of them!
Were I to count them, they would outnumber the grains of sand—
When I awake, I am still with you.
Psalm 139:15-18

I remember wrestling with this Psalm a few years ago. Without realising it, I came to a place in my heart where I had put God into a box in many areas of my life. While I still said I believed that He was far beyond the limits of what I knew and understood, I had begun to doubt this in the way that I lived. I remember reading this scripture and thinking, 'God, you have written out everyday of my life? Your thoughts towards me outnumber the grains of sand? To do that, for even one person, would be an enormous feat. You expect me to believe that you offer that level of intimacy, closeness and detail to every one, including me?'

The voice of the Holy Spirit whispered back to me so gently and lovingly. He simply said, 'Yes. I'm big enough to do that.'

In that second, my whole perspective of who God was began to shift back into its proper place. He is big enough to do that! He has written down every detail of your life, He does have thoughts towards you that outnumber the grains of sand. He did choose you before the foundation of the world and He did predestine you to be found in His son, Jesus. He is big enough to do all that and more! Perhaps, like I did, you may need to take some time over the next few days to readjust your thinking about who God is, to tear down the boxes you have tried to fit him in and to align your thinking with the truth of His word.

Regardless of what you may have been told or may have heard about your birth, you were not a surprise to God. You were not unplanned, not an accident, not a mistake. God was there through it all, from the very beginning. He saw you while you were being put together in your mother's womb. He has seen every day in your life so far – the good, the bad, the ugly and the beautiful! And He is still standing by, still cheering you on and still championing you forwards. He is always thinking of you and His thoughts towards you are good!

PAUSE, PONDER, REFLECT

Questions to Reflect on:
Close your eyes for a few minutes and think on the truth that you are a person so valuable, so special, and so important to God that He was watching while you were formed inside your mother's womb. He has seen every day of your life so far, and has already planned an amazing future for you.

How does this make you feel? Do any thoughts or feelings of inadequacy pop up when you take time to reflect on this truth? If so, write them down and ask the Holy Spirit to help you change your thoughts about yourself so that they line up with the way He feels about you.

How does this truth that you have been predestined add to your value and worth?

Scriptures to Ponder:

Lord, you know everything there is to know about me.
You perceive every movement of my heart and soul,
and you understand my every thought
before it even enters my mind.
You are so intimately aware of me, Lord.
You read my heart like an open book
and you know all the words I'm about to speak
before I even start a sentence!
You know every step I will take before my journey even begins.
You've gone into my future to prepare the way,
and in kindness you follow behind me
to spare me from the harm of my past.
With your hand of love upon my life,
you impart a blessing to me.
This is just too wonderful, deep, and incomprehensible!
Your understanding of me brings me wonder and strength.
Where could I go from your Spirit?
Where could I run and hide from your face?
If I go up to heaven, you're there!
If I go down to the realm of the dead, you're there too!
If I fly with wings into the shining dawn, you're there!
If I fly into the radiant sunset, you're there waiting!
Wherever I go, your hand will guide me;
your strength will empower me.
It's impossible to disappear from you

*or to ask the darkness to hide me,
for your presence is everywhere, bringing light into my night.
There is no such thing as darkness with you.
The night, to you, is as bright as the day;
there's no difference between the two.
You formed my innermost being, shaping my delicate inside
and my intricate outside,
and wove them all together in my mother's womb.
I thank you, God, for making me so mysteriously complex!
Everything you do is marvelously breathtaking.
It simply amazes me to think about it!
How thoroughly you know me, Lord!
You even formed every bone in my body
when you created me in the secret place,
carefully, skillfully shaping me from nothing to something.
You saw who you created me to be before I became me!
Before I'd ever seen the light of day,
the number of days you planned for me
were already recorded in your book.
Every single moment you are thinking of me!
How precious and wonderful to consider
that you cherish me constantly in your every thought!
O God, your desires toward me are more
than the grains of sand on every shore!
When I awake each morning, you're still with me.
Psalm 139:1-18 TPT*

THE IDENTITY PROJECT

YOU WERE PREDESTINED

DAY 18:

YOU HAVE BEEN CHOSEN

'You did not choose Me but I chose you, and appointed you that you might go and bear fruit.' John 15:16 NIV

When we share our experiences of coming to faith, we often say things like 'then I found God'; or 'I chose to follow Jesus'. The truth, however, as we read in the verse above, is that before we made any choice, God chose us. Long before we found Him, He found us.

I once heard someone describe it in this way. Imagine you are lost in a dense forest at night. You have no idea where you are or how to get out. Frantically, you push through the darkness, branches snapping around you and scratching your skin as you desperately search for any sign that you may be close to home. Suddenly, a spotlight illuminates your position and you hear your name called. You begin to make out the fluorescent uniforms of a search and rescue team who have been sent out into the night to search for you. Exhausted, yet relieved, you collapse into their arms and cry out, 'I'm so glad I found you!'

I'm sorry, but in this situation you didn't really do the finding.

You were found. Yes, you were searching. Yes, you were doing everything possible to get out of the darkness. Yes, you were desperately looking for help. But you didn't find the rescue team. They found you.

I have decided that this is a pretty accurate picture of what it was like when I met Jesus. Yes, I was searching. Yes, I had no idea where I was going. Yes, I knew that I needed help. But I didn't find Jesus, even though I thought I had at the time. No, He found me. And this realisation actually makes the gift of salvation all the more beautiful.

And just as He searched for me and found me, He has searched for you and found you. Perhaps even as you have read the pages of this journal! Just as He chose me, He has chosen you. What value and worth your life has!

I love the three stories Jesus tells to illustrate this truth in Luke 15. He begins by telling of a lost sheep and a shepherd who leaves the rest of his flock to find it. This story is followed up by the story of a lost coin and a woman who will not rest until she has found it. Finally, just to really drive home the point, He tells a story of a lost son and a father who waits expectantly for His return.

The truth, my friend, is that you are just as valuable to God the Father as the lost sheep was to the shepherd. Just as precious as the lost coin was to the woman and just as loved as the lost son was by his father. You have great worth and great value.

God chose you long before you choose Him. He found you long before you found Him, and He loved you long before you loved Him in return.

Not only have you been chosen to receive the free gift of salvation and to become a part of God's family, you have also been chosen for a unique, one of a kind, special assignment here on this Earth. We began to explore this idea in our discussions about purpose earlier and will come back to this many times over the coming days. But as part of being chosen, you have also been 'appointed that you would go and bear fruit' (John 15:16). God's design for your life is that you would grow and flourish in the specific calling He has placed within you and gifted you for. More on that soon, but for now, rest in the truth that you have been chosen by a God who loves you.

PAUSE, PONDER, REFLECT

Questions to Reflect on:
Consider your story of coming to faith in Jesus. Do you feel like you found Him, or can you see that really, He was the one working behind the scenes to find you? Take a few minutes to write your story down. It is special, unique and valuable. How does the truth that you have been chosen add value and worth to your identity?

Scriptures to Ponder:
Then Jesus said, "Once there was a father with two sons. The younger son came to his father and said, 'Father, don't you think it's time to give

me the share of your estate that belongs to me?' So the father went ahead and distributed among the two sons their inheritance. Shortly afterward, the younger son packed up all his belongings and travelled off to see the world. He journeyed to a far-off land where he soon wasted all he was given in a binge of extravagant and reckless living.

"With everything spent and nothing left, he grew hungry, for there was a severe famine in that land. So he begged a farmer in that country to hire him. The farmer hired him and sent him out to feed the pigs. The son was so famished; he was willing to even eat the slop given to the pigs, because no one would feed him a thing.

"Humiliated, the son finally realized what he was doing and he thought, 'There are many workers at my father's house who have all the food they want with plenty to spare. They lack nothing. Why am I here dying of hunger, feeding these pigs and eating their slop? I want to go back home to my father's house, and I'll say to him, "Father, I was wrong. I have sinned against you. I'll never be worthy to be called your son. Please, Father, just treat me like one of your employees."'

"So the young son set off for home. From a long distance away, his father saw him coming, dressed as a beggar, and great compassion swelled up in his heart for his son who was returning home. So the father raced out to meet him. He swept him up in his arms, hugged him dearly, and kissed him over and over with tender love.

"Then the son said, 'Father, I was wrong. I have sinned against you. I could never deserve to be called your son. Just let me be—'

"The father interrupted and said, 'Son, you're home now!'

"Turning to his servants, the father said, 'Quick, bring me the best robe, my very own robe, and I will place it on his shoulders. Bring

the ring, the seal of sonship, and I will put it on his finger. And bring out the best shoes you can find for my son. Let's prepare a great feast and celebrate. For this beloved son of mine was once dead, but now he's alive again. Once he was lost, but now he is found!' And everyone celebrated with overflowing joy.'
Luke 15:12-24 TPT

YOU HAVE BEEN CHOSEN

…

DAY 19:

YOU HAVE BEEN REDEEMED

*'They remembered that God was their Rock, that
God Most High was their Redeemer.'*
Psalms 78:35 NIV

Over the next few days, we are going to dive deeply into some big words that you might have heard around church before, but maybe never fully understood. We are also going to look at some Old Testament ways of living, so be prepared to read about a culture that is very different to the one we live in today. We might even unpack some Greek or Hebrew words along the way. All of this will help us to understand what Jesus did at the cross more fully, and, in turn, help us to understand our worth and value as children welcomed into God's family.

So let's get right into unpacking redemption today. When I think about how and when I see this word used in my world, I find it most often in regards to gift vouchers. For example, I might be given a voucher to go to the movies. When I take my voucher to the cinema to redeem it, I hand it over to the attendant and I am given tickets in return. Although they didn't cost me anything, they did cost somebody something. This is the first lesson we learn when we look at redemption. Although salvation is a free gift offered to us, it didn't come cheaply. Jesus paid for our redemption with His life.

When we read the word redemption in the scriptures, it carries a slightly different meaning than it does in our culture today. In the Old Testament, the word *redeem* means to *buy something back, to pay the price required in order to set something free* or to *cover*.[2] To understand how we have truly been *redeemed* at the cross, let's first look at how we got to a state where we needed redemption.

We have already established that God is our creator and that we were designed to be in relationship with Him, living in the fullness of that connection. In the Garden of Eden, however, a great tragedy occurred that separated humanity from God. When Adam and Eve ate the fruit of the forbidden tree in an attempt to become like God, they not only ignored God's voice, but chose to listen to the voice of the serpent instead (you can read the full story in Genesis 3). When God came to look for Adam and Eve in the Garden that afternoon, they were hiding from Him. The shame of their decision had already begun to sink in. You see, in that exchange, they actually chose more than a piece of fruit. They chose a new way. They chose relationship with a new master. And since that day, mankind has been trapped, enslaved by sin, and separated from God. From that day on, we needed to be *redeemed*, to be *bought back*, to be *set free* and *reconnected*.

In His amazing grace, God spilt the blood of a lamb to cover Adam and Eve in their shame and nakedness that day in the Garden (Genesis 3:21). From that point onwards, we see a pattern of animal sacrifice throughout the Old Testament: an innocent animal would be killed in order to cover sin. No animal sacrifice, however, could truly redeem us back to perfect relationship with God. They were merely a temporary covering.

That was until Jesus went to the cross. When He died, as an innocent and perfect person, He paid the full price required for us to be bought back, set free and totally and completely covered. We were redeemed! The door was open for us to enter once again into perfect relationship with God. We no longer belong to the enemy; we belong to God – and what a price He paid to have us back!

This is who you are! You are a person so valuable that Jesus went to the cross, suffered terribly and shed His blood so that the full price could be paid for you to be redeemed.

PAUSE, PONDER, REFLECT

Questions to Reflect on:
How do you feel when you consider that you have been redeemed? What emotions surface in your heart? Write a prayer of thanks as you meditate on this truth. How does this shape your identity? Your worth? Your value?

Scriptures to Ponder:

'For when the time was right, the Anointed One came and died to demonstrate his love for sinners who were entirely helpless, weak, and powerless to save themselves. Now, who of us would dare to die for the sake of a wicked person? We can all understand if someone was willing to die for a truly noble person. But Christ proved God's passionate love for us by dying in our place while we were still lost and ungodly! And there is still much more to say of his unfailing love for us! For through the blood of Jesus we have heard the powerful declaration, "You are now righteous in my sight." And because of the sacrifice of Jesus, you will never experience the wrath of God.'
Romans 5:6-9 TPT

'When Adam sinned, the entire world was affected. Sin entered human experience, and death was the result. And so death followed this sin, casting its shadow over all humanity, because all have sinned.'
Romans 5:12 TPT

'In other words, just as condemnation came upon all people through one transgression, so through one righteous act of Jesus' sacrifice, the perfect righteousness that makes us right with God and leads us to a victorious life is now available to all. One man's disobedience opened the door for all humanity to become sinners. So also one man's obedience opened the door for many to be made perfectly right with God and acceptable to Him. So then, the law was introduced into God's plan to bring the reality of human sinfulness out of hiding.

And yet, wherever sin increased, there was more than enough of God's grace to triumph all the more!' Romans 5:18-20 TPT

THE IDENTITY PROJECT

YOU HAVE BEEN REDEEMED

DAY 20:

YOU HAVE BEEN JUSTIFIED

'And all are justified freely by His grace through the redemption that came by Christ Jesus.' Romans 3:24 NIV

I hope you are ready for another word jam-packed with meaning! We use the word *justify* in our language today, but just as with the word *redeemed*, our use of the word is a little different to the meaning it holds when we read it in the Bible.

In our culture today, we *justify ourselves* by explaining or providing a reason for something we have said or done. It's a word we use to defend ourselves. In the scriptures, however, we read that it is actually *God* who *justifies us!* Let's have a look at the Bible's definition:

'To make righteous, acquit or regard as righteous.' [3]

You may ask, 'What does it mean to be righteous?' Good question. It means to be in *right standing* with God. It means to be clean, to be morally right and upstanding and to be able to enter God's presence. You see, God is completely and utterly pure and holy and you need to be righteous to be able to live with Him in Heaven.

The thing is, however, we aren't righteous. Even on my best day, I am nowhere close to being perfect or holy. When we consider the laws God gave us to live by, even just the 10 Commandments, all of us find that we don't measure up! We have all sinned, all made mistakes, and all fallen short of the expectations of the law.

When Jesus was on the Earth He was asked about the law by people who were struggling to meet all of its many standards, like we do today. He summed up all the laws of the Old Testament in two simple commands. That sounds a bit more achievable, right? Maybe we could get two rules happening in our lives? Have a look at them and see how you measure up:

> 'Jesus answered him, "The first of all the commandments is: 'Hear, O Israel, the Lord our God, the Lord is one. And you shall love the Lord your God with all your heart, with all your soul, with all your mind, and with all your strength.' This is the first commandment. And the second is like it: 'You shall love your neighbour as yourself.' There is no other commandment greater than these."
> Matthew 22:37-40 NIV

I don't know how you went, but again, my life fails to reach the standard. How is it that God can make the declaration over our lives that we are justified and seen as righteous?

Once again, the answer to this question is found in the glory and wonder of the cross. Take a look at how Paul describes it in his book to the Roman Christians:

> *'Since we've compiled this long and sorry record as sinners and proved that we are utterly incapable of living the glorious lives God wills for us, God did it for us. Out of sheer generosity He put us in right standing with Himself. A pure gift. He got us out of the mess we're in and restored us to where He always wanted us to be. And He did it by means of Jesus Christ.'*
> Romans 3:23-24 MSG

I absolutely love the way the Message Bible translates this passage. Simply put, there is no way we could have ever received justification on our own, or have ever been declared righteous based on our own efforts or actions, but God stepped in! Out of sheer love and generosity, He put us in right standing with Himself. All we need to do to receive this justification is believe – we are justified by faith (Romans 3:28).

This is who you are. You are a person so valuable that God did everything required to declare you righteous and justified so you could live the life you were created for.

PAUSE, PONDER, REFLECT

Questions to Reflect on:
How do you feel when you consider that God has declared you as righteous through Jesus? Do you feel that you have to continue to justify yourself? How can you walk differently, talk differently and live differently today considering the truth that God declares righteousness over you?

Scriptures to Ponder:

'For by the merit of observing the law no one earns the status of being declared righteous before God, for it is the law that fully exposes and unmasks the reality of sin. But now, independently of the law, the righteousness of God is tangible and brought to light through Jesus, the Anointed One. This is the righteousness that the Scriptures prophesied would come. It is God's righteousness made visible through the faithfulness of Jesus Christ. And now all who believe in Him receive that gift. For there is really no difference between us, for we all have sinned and are in need of the glory of God. Yet through His powerful declaration of acquittal, God freely gives away his righteousness. His gift of love and favour now cascades over us, all because Jesus, the Anointed One, has liberated us from the guilt, punishment, and power of sin!' Romans 3:20-24 TPT

'We know full well that we don't receive God's perfect righteousness as a reward for keeping the law, but by the faith of Jesus, the Messiah! His faithfulness, not ours, has saved us, and we have received God's perfect righteousness. Now we know that God accepts no one by the keeping of religious laws!'
Ephesians 2:16 TPT

THE IDENTITY PROJECT

YOU HAVE BEEN JUSTIFIED

DAY 21:

YOU HAVE BEEN ADOPTED

*'The Spirit you received does not make you
slaves, so that you live in fear again;
Rather, the Spirit you received brought about your adoption to sonship.
And by Him we cry 'Abba, Father.'
Romans 8:15 NIV*

We are all pretty familiar with the concept of adoption. When we see adoption mentioned in the Bible, it represents a similar process to the one that we are familiar with today. During the time that Paul was writing his letters to the churches, adoption was a legal process by which a Roman citizen could welcome another person, even someone who was held as a slave, into his family.

After the price of adoption was paid, the adopted person was considered to be part of the family in every way – as if they were a biological son or daughter. If the person who was adopted had been a slave, not only were they completely freed from slavery through the process of adoption, but they were also given the privileges and rights of a roman citizen[4].

Adoption works much the same way in our society today. When

adoption takes place, a family chooses to welcome another individual into their home, giving them the same love, care and opportunity that they would to any other member of the family. It's a beautiful and generous choice, with incredible impact on the person who is adopted. Suddenly they have a family again! A place they belong, a place they are loved.

Let's consider this concept in light of what God has done for us. How beautiful is it that we are not simply forgiven when we accept Jesus, but that God opens His arms wide to invite us into His family, adopting us as His sons and daughters. We are a part of His family! And, just as a slave adopted in Rome would inherit all the rights and privileges of Roman citizenship when he was adopted, we have all the rights and privileges of a citizen of Heaven as sons and daughters of God. This is who you are. This is your identity in Christ!

Now, the stand out feature when it comes to adoption is *choice*. When an adoption takes place the *parents* get to *choose* the child who is then welcomed into their family. Most parents who have had biological children might have *chosen* to fall pregnant or planned to start a family, but that is where the choices stop. In the end, they give birth to whomever *God* has *chosen* for them. Those who have been adopted, however, have usually been hand picked by the ones who will adopt them. Consider the fact that God has chosen you to hold a special place in His family. He *wanted* you! And Jesus was willing to go to the cross in order to welcome *you* into God's family.

So what does this mean for our everyday lives? Think about the way you are around your natural family. Often when we are at home, we are most free to simply be ourselves. We walk around in our PJs, with no make up on and our hair a mess. We tell our family how we are really feeling when they ask, and we aren't afraid to speak our minds if we see something that we don't agree with. Family are usually the first people we want to talk to when something amazing happens and the first people we turn to when we experience something terrible. Have you ever considered that as a child of God, adopted fully into His family, you are invited to live with this level of intimacy with your Father in Heaven?

In Romans 8 we are invited to call God *'Abba'* which, in the language of Aramaic, was a familiar name a child would call His father, similar to the way we use the word *'Daddy'* or *'Dad'* in our English language[5]. This is the way God invites you to relate to Him. He invites you to come just as you are. You don't have to be anyone other than yourself when you talk to Him. You can ask Him your most honest questions and tell Him how you are really feeling. He wants to celebrate with you when life is great and be the one you turn to when it is hard. He wants you to live everyday like you are part of His family – because you are!

You are a person so valuable to God that He wanted to adopt you into His family and wants you to call Him your Daddy God. You have been adopted!

PAUSE, PONDER, REFLECT

Questions to Reflect on:
Consider today's truth that you have been adopted into God's family. How does this shape your identity, worth and value? Take a moment to reflect on your experiences with your own family and, in particular, your own father. Chances are that some of your experiences might have been less than perfect – especially considering that all of us are imperfect people. Ask the Holy Spirit to show you if these experiences have impacted your ability to relate to God as a good father. If they have, take some time to write down how these experiences have affected you and place them before God. You may also want to share these experiences with a trusted friend or mentor and ask them to pray with you. Finally, take some time to reflect on the following scriptures that reveal the kind of father that God is. Allow these truths about Him to take root in your heart where lies have been pulled up.

Scriptures to Ponder:

'I will proclaim the Lord's decree:
He said to me, "You are my son; today I have become your father.'
Psalm 2:7 NIV

'Which of you, if your son asks for bread, will give him a stone? Or if he asks for a fish, will give him a snake? If you, then, though you are evil, know how to give good gifts to your children, how much more will your Father in heaven give good gifts to those who ask Him!'
Matthew 7:9-11

'What a God you are! Your path for me has been perfect!
All your promises have proven true.
What a secure shelter for all those who
turn to hide themselves in you!
You are the wrap-around God giving grace to me.
Could there be any other god like you?
You are the only God to be worshiped, for
there is not a more secure foundation
to build my life upon than you.
You have wrapped me in power
and now you've shared with me your perfection.'
Psalm 18:30-32

YOU HAVE BEEN ADOPTED

…

DAY 22:

YOU ARE ROYAL

'But you are a chosen people, a royal priesthood, a holy nation, God's special possession, that you may declare the praises of Him who called you out of darkness into His wonderful light.'
1 Peter 2:9 NIV

Yesterday, we discussed the powerful truth that you have been adopted into the family of God. You are not a slave, not an orphan, not forgotten. Through Jesus, you are a child of God and invited to relate to your Heavenly Father as Daddy God!

While that truth alone adds so much value to our identity, there is more. God loves to do things extravagantly and generously, and when it comes to our identity as His sons and daughters, we have only started to scratch the surface. Today we will remind ourselves that God, who we are invited to call Father, is also a King. In fact, He is the ruler of all the Earth and the King of all the universe. And what do you call the son or daughter of a King?

While the fact that God is all-powerful doesn't change, we can sometimes loose sight of His majesty and greatness when dealing with the realities of day-to-day life. This is why it is so important to develop habits in our lives that point us back to God daily, reminding us of who He is and what He has done for us. This could be as simple as starting each day by reading the Bible, praying on your way to work, or connecting with God through worship. Whatever it might look like for you, reminding yourself of who God is will also remind you of who you are as His child.

Whenever I start to forget that God is the creator and King of everything I see, I love to turn to the book of Job in the Bible. This is one of the oldest books we find in the scriptures and it tells the story of a remarkable man who held onto His trust in God, even when faced with heartbreaking circumstances. If you aren't familiar with the story, Job loses his family and all his wealth in the space of a few days. As per the custom of his time, Job tears his clothes and sits in ashes as he mourns and his friends come to visit him. Now his friends mean well, they offer advice and try to provide possible explanations for why these tragic events have happened in Job's life, and for many of the chapters of this book, we see their conversations recorded. After letting them all have their say, however, God Himself shows up and begins to reveal just how small a box they are trying to put Him in with their limited understanding. He begins by asking them a few simple questions:

> *'Where were you when I laid the earth's*
> *foundation? Tell me, if you understand.*
> *Who marked off its dimensions? Surely you know!*
> *Who stretched a measuring line across it?*
> *On what were its footings set, or who laid its cornerstone—*

> *while the morning stars sang together and*
> *all the angels shouted for joy?'*
> *Job 38:4-7*

Where was I when the world was made? Wow! Suddenly the things I am dealing with don't seem so large. I don't know about you, but I actually find it so reassuring and comforting to be put in my place by these words. It helps me gain perspective.

The God I have given my heart to, the God who invited me into His family and called me His child, truly is in control of everything around me. He is all knowing, all-powerful and ever present. He is my Dad, He is also the King, and I am His child. You are too. So hold your head high my friend and don't let the worries you face today cause you to forget that you are a royal child of God.

PAUSE, PONDER, REFLECT

Questions to Reflect on:
How do you feel when you consider that you are a child of the King of all the universe? Think about the way that we, as humans, strive to always give our best to our children, making sure they are protected and provided for. Does this give you confidence that your Father in Heaven will protect and provide for you? How would you walk, talk and carry yourself if you lived truly believing that you were a royal child of the most high God? What is stopping you from living this way today?

Scriptures to Ponder:

'You will also be [considered] a crown of
glory and splendor in the hand of the Lord,
And a royal diadem [exceedingly beautiful] in the hand of your God.'
Isaiah 63:3

'The Lord is my best friend and my shepherd.
I always have more than enough.
He offers a resting place for me in His luxurious love.
His tracks take me to an oasis of peace, the quiet brook of bliss.
That's where He restores and revives my life.
He opens before me pathways to God's pleasure
and leads me along in his footsteps of righteousness
so that I can bring honor to his name.
Lord, even when your path takes me through the
valley of deepest darkness,
fear will never conquer me, for you already have!
You remain close to me and lead me through it all the way.
Your authority is my strength and my peace.
The comfort of your love takes away my fear.
I'll never be lonely, for you are near.
You become my delicious feast
even when my enemies dare to fight.
You anoint me with the fragrance of your Holy Spirit;
you give me all I can drink of you until my heart overflows.
So why would I fear the future?
For your goodness and love pursue me all the days of my life.

YOU ARE ROYAL

*Then afterward, when my life is through,
I'll return to your glorious presence to be forever with you!'
Psalm 23 TPT*

THE IDENTITY PROJECT

YOU ARE ROYAL

DAY 23:

YOU HAVE AN INHERITANCE

'I pray that the eyes of your heart may be enlightened in order that you may know the hope to which He has called you, the riches of His glorious inheritance in His holy people.'
Ephesians 1:18 NIV

By now I hope you are starting to realise that when God adopted us into His family, He invited us in 100 percent. We are sons and daughters through and through, fully welcomed into the family, royal children of the King. Today we will discover that God even goes as far as to include us as heirs in the family inheritance!

You may be thinking, 'Well, that sounds pretty good, but what exactly is this inheritance?' Great question! A large part of the inheritance that the Bible mentions for those who believe in Jesus is eternal – a life in Heaven with God when we leave this Earth. Yet there is also a large aspect of our inheritance that we are invited to step into here on Earth.

You see, Jesus didn't go to the cross so that you could struggle through life and just scrape into Heaven. When God opened the door wide to welcome you into His family, He also invited you to live a life flourishing in every area.

> *'For if, by the trespass of the one man, death reigned through that one man, how much more will those who receive God's abundant provision of grace and of the gift of righteousness reign in life through the one man, Jesus Christ!'*
> Romans 5:17 NIV

Just as we inherited sin and death through Adam's choice in the garden, we inherit righteousness and the opportunity to *reign in life* through Jesus. This word *reign* means to rule or have authority, just as a King reigns over his kingdom. Put simply, this scripture is saying that it is God's desire for you to be *thriving* in all areas of your life – in your health, in your well being, in your family, in your relationships, in your workplace, in your finances, and any other area you can think of! God cares about you as a whole person – physically, spiritually and emotionally. Through Jesus you are called to reign and thrive in every area of life. This is your inheritance as a child of God.

Now I have found that the most important area of our lives to be experiencing the grace and abundance of this inheritance is in our internal world: our heart, our mind and our emotions. Everything else in life flows from this part of our lives, and sooner or later, the state of our heart will be reflected in the world we create around us. I have found in my own life that even when things feel like they are falling apart around me, if I can keep peace in my heart and not allow my mind to become worried or anxious, I can continue to walk on, one day at a time, with confidence that everything will eventually fall into place. Whatever I am facing, I can still walk in my inheritance to reign in life.

Jesus was a perfect example of this. In Mark 4, when He and His disciples found themselves at sea during a storm, Jesus had no trouble sleeping on the boat. When His disciples woke Him up, He had no trouble speaking the peace that He held in His heart out into the atmosphere, and soon enough the storm had calmed. Now that's what I call reigning in life – and Jesus invites each one of us to live from this place.

> 'Peace I leave with you; my peace I give you. I do not give to you as the world gives. Do not let your hearts be troubled and do not be afraid.'
> John 14:27 NIV

This is who you are. You are a person so valuable that God Himself has invited you to share in an eternal inheritance and reign in life through Jesus. It is your right as His child to live with peace, health and provision in every area of your life!

PAUSE, PONDER, REFLECT

Questions to Reflect on:
Jesus promised us peace and invited us not to be troubled or afraid. How does this compare with the current status of your heart, soul and mind? Are you living in the inheritance that Jesus died to give you?
Consider some other areas of your life such as your family, relationships, work, finances and health. Do you feel that you are thriving and reigning in these areas? Place each area before God

and ask Him to show you what steps you need to take to walk in your inheritance. You may also want to ask God to bring people into your world that can guide and mentor you in learning to understand and apply God's Kingdom principles when it comes to giving, stewarding your time and abilities well, and walking in grace and forgiveness.

Scriptures to Ponder

'At one time we too were foolish, disobedient, deceived and enslaved by all kinds of passions and pleasures. We lived in malice and envy, being hated and hating one another. But when the kindness and love of God our Saviour appeared, He saved us, not because of righteous things we had done, but because of His mercy. He saved us through the washing of rebirth and renewal by the Holy Spirit, whom He poured out on us generously through Jesus Christ our Saviour, so that, having been justified by His grace, we might become heirs having the hope of eternal life.'
Titus 3:3-7 NIV

"No weapon that is formed against you will succeed; And every tongue that rises against you in judgment you will condemn. This [peace, righteousness, security, and triumph over opposition] is the heritage of the servants of the Lord, and this is their vindication from Me," says the Lord.
Isaiah 54:17 AMP

'Your hearts can soar with joyful gratitude when you think of how God made you worthy to receive the glorious inheritance freely given

to us by living in the light. He has rescued us completely from the tyrannical rule of darkness and has translated us into the kingdom realm of his beloved Son. For in the Son all our sins are cancelled and we have the release of redemption through His very blood.'
Colossians 3:12-14 TPT

YOU HAVE AN INHERITANCE

THE IDENTITY PROJECT

DAY 24:

YOU ARE CALLED

'He has saved us and called us to a holy life - not because of anything we have done but because of His own purpose and grace. This grace was given us in Christ Jesus before the beginning of time.'
2 Timothy 1:9 NIV

Let's pause for a moment and reflect on the second layer of identity that we have been building over the last week. We began by considering the truth that we have been predestined and chosen by God. Regardless of what you may have heard about your life, it was not an accident or a mistake in God's books. We then looked at the amazing love and grace that was displayed when Jesus went to the cross. While we were lost in sin, Jesus paid the full price required for our redemption. Although we could never deserve it or earn it, God declared us justified and righteous through the blood of Jesus. As if that was not enough, He then opened wide the doors of His family to us, adopting us as His royal sons and daughters, with full access to HIs glorious inheritance and the invitation to know Him intimately as our Daddy God.

And we are still not finished! We have two more significant stones to put in place as we finish building this vital layer of our identity. Today we will look at the truth that God has *called* each one of us to live a life of holiness and purpose.

From cover to cover, the Bible is full of stories of ordinary people who were called by God to do extraordinary things. Noah was called to build an ark, Abraham was called to leave the land he knew, Joseph was called to save all of Egypt from famine, Moses was called to deliver God's people from slavery, and we haven't even left Genesis yet! From Joshua to the prophets, from the disciples and the apostle Paul, God's call can be seen throughout all of the scriptures. And His voice still calls to us today – if we are willing to recognise and respond to it.

Firstly, we are called in this life to become like Jesus. In the book of Ephesians Paul encourages us to put on our 'new self', which is made in the likeness of God, and later to be imitators of God (Ephesians 4:22, 5:1). To imitate someone well you have to know them well. This calling is really a call to intimacy, a call to know God so deeply that we cannot help but become like Him.

> *'Now the Lord is the Spirit, and where the Spirit of the Lord is, there is freedom. And we all, who with unveiled faces contemplate the Lord's glory, are being transformed into his image with ever-increasing glory.'*
> *2 Corinthians 3:17-18 NIV*

This is our first and highest calling in life. In many ways it reflects what Jesus identified as the greatest commandment:

> *To love the Lord with all your heart, all your soul, all your mind and all your strength (Luke 12:29-31).*

Our second calling in life, in a similar way, reflects Jesus' second commandment: To love your neighbour as yourself. The second calling we receive in life is to be a part of God's answer for humanity – to play a role in revealing the unconditional love of God to those around us. Now, this may look vastly different for each one of us, depending on our own individual strengths, gifts, talents and passions, but what an honour and privilege it is to be called by God to be a part of His story on the Earth! He *wants you* on His team and has a special role He has called you to play. Isn't that an awesome truth to ponder today! I don't know about you, but I think that adds great worth and value to your identity.

PAUSE, PONDER, REFLECT

Questions to Reflect on:
God has called you to become like Jesus and to partner with Him in showing His love to the world. How does this make you feel? How does this change the way you see yourself? How does this change the way you see your purpose?

Scriptures to Ponder:
> *'You did not choose me, but I chose you and appointed you so that you might go and bear fruit – fruit that will last – and so that whatever you ask in my name the Father*

will give you. This is my command: Love each other.'
John 15:16-17 NIV

'And we know [with great confidence] that God [who is deeply concerned about us] causes all things to work together [as a plan] for good for those who love God, to those who are called according to His plan and purpose.'
Romans 8:28 AMP

'I admit that I haven't yet acquired the absolute fullness that I'm pursuing, but I run with passion into His abundance so that I may reach the purpose that Jesus Christ has called me to fulfil and wants me to discover. I don't depend on my own strength to accomplish this; however I do have one compelling focus: I forget all of the past as I fasten my heart to the future instead. I run straight for the divine invitation of reaching the heavenly goal and gaining the victory-prize through the anointing of Jesus. So let all who are fully mature have this same passion, and if anyone is not yet gripped by these desires, God will reveal it to them. And let us all advance together to reach this victory-prize, following one path with one passion.'
Philippians 4:12-16 TPT

YOU ARE CALLED

THE IDENTITY PROJECT

DAY 25:
YOU ARE EMPOWERED

'But you will receive power when the Holy Spirit comes on you; and you will be my witnesses in Jerusalem, and in all Judea and Samaria, and to the ends of the earth.'
Acts 1:8 NIV

We have one more stone to lay today in the foundation we are building of our identity as a part of God's family. In many ways, you could say that we have left the best till last, as God's gift of the Holy Spirit empowers and transforms every area of our lives, truly giving us the ability to live in the fullness of God's best for us! Let's get straight into it.

Firstly, let's look at who the Holy Spirit is. He is a part of the Trinity and exists in perfect unity and relationship with God the Father and Jesus the Son. It was the Holy Spirit who hovered above the surface of Earth when God began to create the world in Genesis 1, and it was the Holy Spirit that Jesus promised to send before He left the Earth. The Holy Spirit is a great counsellor, teacher and guide (John 14:26). He leads us into truth and help us to become discerning (John 16:13), and He empowers us to minister just as Jesus did (Acts 1:8).

When the Holy Spirit first arrived He made quite an entrance! In Acts 2, while the disciples were meeting together in prayer, He came as the sound of rushing wind and flames of fire came to rest on the heads of all those in the room. The Holy Spirit empowered those who received Him to do extraordinary things, including the ability to speak in other tongues. Peter got up that same day and preached an incredible message that moved over 3000 people to follow Jesus (Acts 2:14). In the very next chapter, Peter and John, while on the way to the temple, healed a man who had been lame from birth (Acts 3:1-10).

The rest of the book of Acts records how the message of Jesus exploded through the Earth as people who were filled with the Holy Spirit went out and transformed people's lives and influenced whole communities. People were healed both physically and emotionally and others were set free from oppressive spirits. Many had their dignity restored and their eyes opened to truth when they encountered God's presence on His people. God's plan to draw people back to lives of wholeness and into perfect relationship with Himself unfolded rapidly with the arrival of the Holy Spirit.

Did you know that the Holy Spirit's role in the Earth today hasn't changed? He is still here to empower followers of Jesus to influence and transform the world around them with the love of God.

You see, the Holy Spirit brings life and joy to our lives. He activates the gifts God has placed within us, making us an effective witness for Christ. The Holy Spirit brings revelation to us as we read God's Word. He guides us into truth, teaches us and leads us. The Holy Spirit transforms us and empowers us to live a life worthy of the price that Jesus paid on the cross. It is the Holy Spirit that enables us to become more like Jesus, to develop the fruit of the Spirit in our lives and to fulfill the plans and purposes God has for us. You cannot afford to be without Him if you want to live in the fullness of all God has for your life – and the good news is that you don't have to be! The baptism of the Holy Spirit is available for every believer.

This is your identity. This is part of who you are. You are a person so valuable, so significant to God that He has sent His Holy Spirit to dwell in you, empower you, lead you and guide you into all that He has planned for your life.

PAUSE, PONDER, REFLECT

Questions to Reflect on:
Have you received the Holy Spirit? Talk with a trusted friend or mentor and ask them to pray with you to receive Him into your life. If you have already received the Holy Spirit, invite Him to empower your life in a fresh way today. Spend some time worshiping and praying in tongues and write down anything God brings to your attention or puts on your heart.

Scriptures to Ponder:

'Jesus replied, "Loving me empowers you to obey my word. And my Father will love you so deeply that we will come to you and make you our dwelling place. But those who don't love me will not obey my words. The Father did not send me to speak my own revelation, but the words of my Father. I am telling you this while I am still with you. But when the Father sends the Spirit of Holiness, the One like me who sets you free, He will teach you all things in my name. And He will inspire you to remember every word that I've told you.

"I leave the gift of peace with you – my peace. Not the kind of fragile peace given by the world, but my perfect peace. Don't yield to fear or be troubled in your hearts – instead, be courageous!"'

John 14:23-27 TPT

'There is so much more I would like to say to you, but it's more than you can grasp at this moment. But when the truth-giving Spirit comes, He will unveil the reality of every truth within you. He won't speak his own message, but only what He hears from the Father, and He will reveal prophetically to you what is to come. He will glorify me on the earth, for He will receive from me what is mine and reveal it to you. Everything that belongs to the Father belongs to me—that's why I say that the Divine Encourager will receive what is mine and reveal it to you. Soon you won't see me any longer, but then, after a little while, you will see me in a new way.'

John 16:12-16 TPT

'On the day Pentecost was being fulfilled, all the disciples were gathered in one place. Suddenly they heard the sound of a violent blast of wind rushing into the house from out of the heavenly realm. The roar of the wind was so overpowering it was all anyone could bear! Then all at once a pillar of fire appeared before their eyes. It separated into tongues of fire that engulfed each one of them. They were all filled and equipped with the Holy Spirit and were inspired to speak in tongues - empowered by the Spirit to speak in languages they had never learned!'
Acts 2:1-4 TPT

THE IDENTITY PROJECT

YOU ARE EMPOWERED

DAY 26:

I CAN DO ALL THINGS

'I can do all things through Christ who strengthens me.'
Philippians 4:13 NKJV

In the scripture listed above, the Apostle Paul boldly declares 'I can do all things through Christ who strengthens me.' He makes this statement after sharing with the Philippian church that he had learned to be content in every situation: good times, hard times, times of abundance and times of struggle. And let me tell you – Paul knew what it was to experience a challenge! During his time as a follower of Jesus, he was imprisoned multiple times, often unjustly. He was in a storm at sea that was so severe the ship he was travelling in was shipwrecked and he and the others with him ended up swimming to an island. And eventually, Paul died as a martyr in Rome. Yet despite all of this, he wrote many times to encourage other followers of Jesus to be joyful and content, regardless of the circumstances of their lives! How did Paul get to this place of confidence? I believe it came from truly knowing and understanding his identity, including who he was in Christ.

Paul knew he had been chosen. He knew he had been redeemed and justified by the cross. He knew he had been adopted into

God's family, given a blessed inheritance and he was filled with the Holy Spirit. Paul knew his born-again identity! He knew who he was as someone found in God's family.

We have considered the importance of building strong foundations a few times already in this journal. The truth is that in life you will face your own storms and struggles, just as Paul did. There will be good times and hard times. How well you make it through life's storms will depend on the foundation you choose to build in your life. Trees with well-established root systems survive storms. Paul was able to face whatever came his way with confidence because he was sure and secure in his identity in Christ. You can be too!

Remember the words of Jesus; He gave us some excellent wisdom about how to build your life on a strong foundation:

> 'Therefore whoever hears these sayings of Mine, and does them, I will liken him to a wise man who built his house on the rock: and the rain descended, the floods came, and the winds blew and beat on that house; and it did not fall, for it was founded on the rock. But everyone who hears these sayings of Mine, and does not do them, will be like a foolish man who built his house on the sand: and the rain descended, the floods came, and the winds blew and beat on that house; and it fell. And great was its fall.'
> Matthew 7:24-27

The surest foundation you can build is one based on what Jesus has said. When it comes to your identity and what you believe about yourself, don't take anyone else's opinion into account! Instead, build it on what God says about you.

To begin with, He created you in His image. You are spiritual, creative, intelligent, able to communicate, relational and formed with a moral compass and sense of purpose. On top of that, you were chosen and predestined to be here on the Earth at this point in time. You are not a mistake! And finally, through His son, Jesus, God sees you as redeemed, justified, adopted, royal, called and blessed with a glorious inheritance, not to mention empowered by Holy Spirit!

This is who you are. This is your identity as someone created in the image of God and found in Christ, and through Him, you can do all things! You can thrive in any circumstance, you can grow through any challenge; you can live a life grounded in peace and joy, regardless of what life looks like around you. This is the life you are invited to walk in through Jesus!

Believe it or not, there is actually still more to discover about who God has created you to be, but today, let's pause and meditate on what we have discovered so far.

PAUSE, PONDER, REFLECT

Questions to Reflect on:
How do you feel when you reflect on what we have discussed about your identity over the last few weeks? Do these truths clash with some of the thoughts you currently believe about yourself? What

areas of your identity need adjusting? Ask God to help rebuild the foundations of your identity as you reflect on who He is and what He has said about you.

Scripture to Ponder:

'Be cheerful with joyous celebration in every season of life. Let joy overflow, for you are united with the Anointed One! Let gentleness be seen in every relationship, for our Lord is ever near. Don't be pulled in different directions or worried about a thing. Be saturated in prayer throughout each day, offering your faith-filled requests before God with overflowing gratitude. Tell Him every detail of your life, then God's wonderful peace that transcends human understanding, will make the answers known to you through Jesus Christ. So keep your thoughts continually fixed on all that is authentic and real, honorable and admirable, beautiful and respectful, pure and holy, merciful and kind. And fasten your thoughts on every glorious work of God, praising Him always. Follow the example of all that we have imparted to you and the God of peace will be with you in all things. My heart overflows with joy when I think of how you showed your love to me by your financial support of my ministry. For even though you have so little, you still continue to help me at every opportunity. I'm not telling you this because I'm in need, for I have learned to be satisfied in any circumstance. I know what it means to lack, and I know what it means to experience overwhelming abundance. For I'm trained in the secret of overcoming all things, whether in fullness or in hunger. And I find that the strength of Christ's explosive power infuses me to conquer every difficulty.'

Philippians 4:5-13 TPT

THE IDENTITY PROJECT

I CAN DO ALL THINGS

PART THREE

gifted

FOR

greatness

— YOUR IDENTITY AS A UNIQUELY
GIFTED INDIVIDUAL —

DAY 27:

STIR IT UP

'For this reason I remind you to fan into flame the gift of God, which is in you through the laying on of my hands. For the Spirit God gave us does not make us timid, but gives us power, love and self-discipline.'
2 Timothy 1:6-7 NIV

I hope and pray that some major construction has taken place in your heart over the last few weeks as we have begun to build a strong and solid identity, based on truth. Remember that our goal on this journey is to build an identity that becomes an unshakable foundation for a strong life, not a foundation that shifts and cracks with the pressures that come our way.

In order to do this, we want to build a foundation that is deep. In the same way that deep roots will hold a large tree firmly in the ground, even through a storm, an identity that is deeply rooted in the truth of what God says about you will hold you firmly in place, even through crisis and challenge. To do this we are going to build four layers of foundation into our identity. We have already built the first two by discovering what it really means to be made in the image of God, and then our identity in Christ, and we have another exciting two layers to go!

The rest of our journey will be a whole lot more personal. While the first two layers we have examined hold powerful truths to build your life on, they are not exactly unique. The first layer, based on the truth that you are made in the image of God, applies to every single human being that God has created. It is still amazing, but amazing for everyone. The second layer, based on the truth of who you are in Christ, applies to everyone who has accepted the free gift of salvation through Jesus. It is also amazing! But again, amazing for everyone. The truth is that we are all incredibly unique and individual, right down to our fingerprints! And our identities should reflect this. So the next two layers we build into our foundation will get right into how God has gifted and purposed each of us uniquely as one-of-a-kind individuals.

Our scripture for today is taken from a letter that Paul the apostle wrote to Timothy, encouraging him to 'fan into flame' the gifts that were on his life (2 Timothy 1:6). Paul saw Timothy as a spiritual son and wrote to encourage him to step into the fullness of his destiny in Christ. I hope that the next few pages of this journal will do that for you. I love the picture this scripture paints of the gifts on our lives being like a small fire that can be fanned into a larger flame. Fire can bring so much warmth and light into the world if it is managed in the right way. If, however, it is allowed to run wild and uncontrolled, it can cause great pain and damage, and if it is neglected it can be reduced to a small pile of cooling coals.

In the same way, the gifts God has placed within each of us have been put there to bring light and warmth to the world around us.

If we steward them in the right way they will grow to produce joy and life, wherever we find ourselves. However, just as they have the power to bring great good to the world, they also have the power to cause great harm if we misuse them and can dwindle away to nothing if we neglect and bury them.

Over the coming days we will look at some of the different aspects of our uniqueness and individuality. We will consider how our personalities, love languages, spiritual giftings, skills, talents and passions are all different, and how all of these different elements work together to form the third layer of our identity as unique individuals.

PAUSE, PONDER, REFLECT

Questions to Reflect on:
Consider the truth that God has uniquely and individually gifted you for greatness. How does this make you feel? Think about your strengths and the things you are passionate about. How have these strengths and gifts on your life been stewarded so far? Have they been encouraged, neglected, or perhaps misused? How do you think they form part of your unique identity? How do they influence the way you see yourself?

Scriptures to Ponder:
'So, my very dear friends, don't get thrown off course. Every desirable and beneficial gift comes out of heaven. The gifts are rivers of light cascading down from the Father of Light. There is nothing deceitful

in God, nothing two-faced, nothing fickle. He brought us to life using the true Word, showing us off as the crown of all His creatures.'
James 1:16-18 MSG

'Just as each one of you has received a special gift [a spiritual talent, an ability graciously given by God], employ it in serving one another as [is appropriate for] good stewards of God's multi-faceted grace [faithfully using the diverse, varied gifts and abilities granted to Christians by God's unmerited favour].'
1 Peter 4:10 AMP

'That is why I remind you to fan into flame the gracious gift of God, [that inner fire - the special endowment] which is in you through the laying on of my hands [with those of the elders at your ordination]. For God did not give us a spirit of timidity or cowardice or fear, but [He has given us a spirit] of power and of love and of sound judgment and personal discipline [abilities that result in a calm, well-balanced mind and self-control].'
2 Timothy 1:6-7 AMP

THE IDENTITY PROJECT

STIR IT UP

DAY 28:

YOUR PERSONALITY

*'I praise you, for I am fearfully and wonderfully made.
Wonderful are Your works; my soul knows it very well.'*
Psalm 139:14 ESV

I'm certain that whatever your experiences have been so far in life, you would agree with the statement that people are different. We think differently, we react to situations differently and we all experience emotions differently. There is no one else out there exactly like you.

As we dive into this third section of our journal today, we will be starting to get really personal, looking at just how uniquely and individually God has created you – and we are going to start by looking at personality. There is no one else on Earth with a personality exactly like yours. While some personalities might be similar, no two are exactly the same. Some of us are people orientated, while others are task driven. Some of us are able to naturally lead and inspire and others find themselves most at home in a supporting or steady role. Some of us are introverts and thinkers, valuing one-on-one conversation over a crowd, while others are extraverts, wearing their hearts on their sleeves and always enjoying the company of others. Our personalities are as varied and different as our fingerprints; God has truly designed each of us uniquely and individually! Right down to the way we think, feel and process the world.

Whatever your personality looks like, we are going to begin today by revisiting the truth that you have been fearfully and wonderfully made by a God who loves you. This truth must ground, guard and guide any discussion we have about our unique differences, strengths and weaknesses. In fact, this is why this journal has been carefully structured to spend a lot of time building a strong foundation on the truth that we are people created in the image of God and found in His family, before beginning to look at the things that make us unique. You see, all of us have a natural tendency to compare when we explore subjects like this, which is not a very healthy activity for the soul. So before we get started, take a moment to reflect on the truth that you have been carefully woven together by a God who loves you, and regardless of what others may have said about your personality, or what you currently think or feel about your personality, God thought the world needed someone wired exactly the way you are!

So, from this perspective, let's look at personality. The fact that God has created each of us differently is amazing and leads to so much creativity and diversity in the world. Just think what a boring place it would be if we were all the same! Diversity, however, does also bring us unique challenges, including the need to recognise and empathise with the differences of others. The more we can learn about how different personalities function, the better we will begin to understand ourselves and those around us.

The complexities of personality and the way people think, feel and respond to the world around them has been the subject of study for hundreds of years. People have been curious about understanding themselves and each other for a long time. One of my favourite researchers in this area was an American Psychologist of the 1920's named William Moulton Marston. He was also an inventor and in his spare time, created the *Wonder Woman* comics.[6] A cool guy if you ask me! Dr Marston's research suggested that there are four distinct personality styles and that your own individual personality is a blend of the four. Over the years, many other personality theories and frameworks have built on and expanded the work of Marston and other psychologists in this field. It is such a large area of research that I could not possibly go into adequate detail or description of them on these limited pages. But, understanding your unique personality is incredibly important.

So, there is some work for you to complete online today in this area. If you haven't already, please visit our online community at www.identityproject.com.au. This is a great interactive platform where you can connect with others who are on the journey of building a strong, truth-centred identity. And, if you follow the links to 'Gifted for Greatness', you will find a whole lot more information on personality types, as well as some links you can follow to take a free personality quiz. This will give you a far more personal and in depth look at your unique personality than I can give you here. Have fun!

PAUSE, PONDER, REFLECT

Questions to Reflect on:
What did you find out about your personality style? Do you feel that the strengths and weaknesses described in your results are an accurate reflection of you? If you have time, do some reading on the other styles of personality and reflect on the traits you see in the people closest to you. Do you feel you are better equipped to understand and support them with this knowledge and insight into their unique personalities?

Scriptures to Ponder:
'It is through Him that we live and function and have our identity; just as your own poets have said, "Our lineage comes from him." '
Acts 17:28 TPT

'Finally, believers, whatever is true, whatever is honourable and worthy of respect, whatever is right and confirmed by God's word, whatever is pure and wholesome, whatever is lovely and brings peace, whatever is admirable and of good repute; if there is any excellence, if there is anything worthy of praise, think continually on these things [centre your mind on them, and implant them in your heart]. The things which you have learned and received and heard and seen in me, practice these things [in daily life], and the God

[who is the source] of peace and well-being will be with you.'
Philippians 4:8-9 AMP

'But that's not all! Even in times of trouble we have a joyful confidence, knowing that our pressures will develop in us patient endurance. And patient endurance will refine our character, and proven character leads us back to hope. And this hope is not a disappointing fantasy, because we can now experience the endless love of God cascading into our hearts through the Holy Spirit who lives in us!'
Romans 5:3-5 TPT

YOUR PERSONALITY

THE IDENTITY PROJECT

DAY 29:

YOUR LOVE LANGUAGE

'Beloved, let us love one another, for love is from God, and whoever loves has been born of God and knows God… because God is love.'
1 John 4:7-8 NIV

The Bible tells us that God is love. Not just that He *is loving*, but that He *is love*. He is the complete and total embodiment of the powerful force we call love, and, as someone created in His image, you have been designed to feel and experience love too. How beautiful is that! Just think for a moment how different the world would look without it. I don't know about you, but I am so glad that God gave us the ability to feel and experience love.

As we discussed yesterday, God has created each of us differently, and as a result of this, each of us actually give, receive and experience love in slightly different ways. The things that make one person feel loved and special can mean nothing to another. Dr Gary Chapman describes this aspect of love so simply in his best selling book titled 'The Five Love Languages'[7]. Totally worth a read. We are going to explore briefly these five languages today, as the way we each give and receive love forms another huge part of our unique and individual identity.

Similar to the way that petrol fuels a car, love fuels our relationships. If there is no petrol in your car, you won't expect to get very far. In the same way, if there is no 'love in the tank', our relationships stop moving forward. Because we all give and receive love in different ways, it is actually possible to be in a loving relationship, yet *feel* unloved. This is where the five love languages can become incredibly valuable. By learning to understand the way we each give and receive love differently, we can come to better understand ourselves and those around us. Let's take a look at them together.

Words of Affirmation is the first of the five love languages. If a person's primary love language is words of affirmation, they need to *hear* affirming and encouraging words in order to *feel* loved. This person may feel more loved receiving a beautiful note or a message than they will receiving an expensive gift without a card. Because words play such a large role in how they give and receive love, people who identify with this love language may also feel *unloved* if they are spoken to in a way that is harsh or demanding.

Quality Time is the second of the five love languages. A person whose primary love language is quality time will feel loved and valued when they are given time and attention from the people who love them. Giving your undivided attention is what really counts for a person who gives and receives love in this way, as well as quality conversations. A person whose primary love language is quality time may feel unloved if you rush through conversations with them, or appear distracted or keen to move on when spending time with them.

Receiving Gifts is the third love language. Gifts are one of the oldest and most beautiful ways a person can express or show their love for someone. For a person whose primary love language is receiving gifts, the value of the gift is not as important as the fact that a gift was given. Gifts say to a person, 'I care about you, and I was thinking about you while we were apart.' Gifts also become symbols of a relationship, reminding the person about the giver of the gift, and the occasion or moment that the gift was given.

Acts of Service is the fourth love language. People who speak this love language feel loved and valued when they are given practical help from another person. Believe it or not, simple, practical things like mowing the lawn, washing the dishes, taking the garbage out or feeding the dog can be ways of saying 'I love you and I care about you!' Acts of service put love into action, and as a result leave the person being served feeling loved and valued.

Physical Touch is the fifth love language. I'm sure each of us have experienced how powerful physical touch can be in communicating love and value. Even very young children who cannot yet understand or speak a language can understand and respond to the language of love through touch. Hugs, kisses, holding hands, high-fives, sitting close to someone, resting your hand on their shoulder, or putting your arm around them are all ways that physical touch can be used to communicate love and value to a person.

You may have already identified your primary love language just by reading this. Chances are that as you read the descriptions of the love languages above, you thought 'That's me! That's exactly what I'm like!' You may have thought that about more than one of the love languages and that's okay too. Once again, there is not enough space in these pages to give you as much information as I would like to on this amazing topic. If you want to learn more about the 5 love languages, and take a quiz to help you determine your own language, jump online at www.identityproject.com.au and follow the links to 'Gifted for Greatness'.

PAUSE, PONDER, REFLECT

Questions to Reflect on:
What is your primary love language? Do you feel that the strengths and weaknesses described are an accurate reflection of you? If you have time, do some reading on the other love languages and reflect on the traits you see in the people closest to you. What things have your learnt today about the love languages of those close to you? Do you feel you are better equipped to understand and support them with this knowledge?

Scriptures to Ponder:
The Way of Love:
'If I speak in the tongues of men or of angels, but do not have love, I am only a resounding gong or a clanging cymbal. If I have the gift of prophecy and can fathom all mysteries and all knowledge, and if

I have a faith that can move mountains, but do not have love, I am nothing. If I give all I possess to the poor and give over my body to hardship that I may boast, but do not have love, I gain nothing. Love is patient, love is kind. It does not envy, it does not boast, it is not proud. It does not dishonour others, it is not self-seeking, it is not easily angered, it keeps no record of wrongs. Love does not delight in evil but rejoices with the truth. It always protects, always trusts, always hopes, always perseveres. Love never fails. But where there are prophecies, they will cease; where there are tongues, they will be stilled; where there is knowledge, it will pass away. For we know in part and we prophesy in part, but when completeness comes, what is in part disappears. When I was a child, I talked like a child, I thought like a child, I reasoned like a child. When I became a man, I put the ways of childhood behind me. For now we see only a reflection as in a mirror; then we shall see face to face. Now I know in part; then I shall know fully, even as I am fully known. And now these three remain: faith, hope and love. But the greatest of these is love.'

1 Corinthians 13:1-13 NIV

THE IDENTITY PROJECT

YOUR LOVE LANGUAGE

DAY 30:

YOUR SPIRITUAL GIFTS

'There are different kinds of gifts, but the same Spirit distributes them. There are different kinds of service, but the same Lord. There are different kinds of working, but in all of them and in everyone it is the same God at work.'
1 Corinthians 12:4-6 NIV

I hope that you are finding it helpful and valuable to discover just how uniquely and individually you have been created – right down to your personality and the way you feel and experience love. There is still more to come in forming this layer of your identity. Today we will look at your unique spiritual gifts.

Spiritual gifts are referred to throughout the writings of the New Testament. They are simply different ways that God has gifted or empowered you to share His message of love, hope and grace to the world around you. God has called each one of us to be a part of His plan on the Earth, and He has given us everything we need to fulfil our specific role. Let's take a look at some of the gifts that are listed in the book of Romans. You may see some of your strengths as you read through this passage.

> *'For just as each of us has one body with many members, and these members do not all have the same function, so in Christ we, though many, form one body, and each member belongs to all the others. We have different gifts, according to the grace given to each of us. If your gift is prophesying, then prophesy in accordance with your faith; if it is serving, then serve; if it is teaching, then teach; if it is to encourage, then give encouragement; if it is giving, then give generously; if it is to lead, do it diligently; if it is to show mercy, do it cheerfully.'*
> Romans 12:4-8

Paul lists seven gifts of the spirit in this passage of scripture, all of which are important and needed in the world today. These gifts include the ability to prophecy, the desire to serve others, the ability to teach and the desire to encourage and build others up. The gift of generosity and the ability to lead are also mentioned as gifts of the spirit, as with the ability to show mercy and compassion to others. In 1 Corinthians 12, other gifts including words of knowledge, faith, discernment, miracles and interpreting tongues are also listed.

The spiritual gifts listed in both of these passages are desperately needed in our world today and should be valued and nurtured in each of our lives. The gifts placed on your life have been entrusted to you by your Father in Heaven because they are needed here in on Earth. How significant is that!

I love that Paul uses the analogy of a body when he talks about the gifts of the spirit. To me, it highlights how important it is that we acknowledge, appreciate and value the fact that we are all different. We need to be! A body is made up of thousands of different and unique tissues, fibres, organs, structures and systems and cannot exist in a healthy state unless each individual part is able to function the way it was designed to. In the same way, the 'body of Christ' is made up of millions of unique and different individuals. Just like a physical body, it is only able to operate effectively and create lasting change in the world when each member understands his or her unique place and gifting. There is no room for comparison or jealousy here. These time wasters only cause pain and slow down the work we are called to do and the destiny each of us has been designed to fulfil.

Just as with our personality styles and love languages, you may have felt you resonated with one or more of these gifts as you read through the scripture from Romans listed above. That's great! If you didn't, or if you would like to read about each of the spiritual gifts in more detail, you can head online to www.identityproject.com.au to complete a free online analysis. Again, follow the links to the 'Gifted for Greatness' page. This is a huge part of your identity; you have been uniquely gifted by God to be a part of His plan to bring hope and wholeness to all people.

PAUSE, PONDER, REFLECT

Questions to Reflect on:
What are your spiritual gifts? Have you had any experiences or opportunities in your life to use this gift? Do you feel that it comes

naturally to you? What might you need to do to grow this gift in your life?

Scriptures to Ponder:
'The same God distributes different kinds of miracles that accomplish different results through each believer's gift and ministry as he energizes and activates them. Each believer is given continuous revelation by the Holy Spirit to benefit not just himself but all.
For example:
The Spirit gives to one the gift of the word of wisdom.
To another, the same Spirit gives the gift of
the word of revelation knowledge.
And to another, the same Spirit gives the gift of faith.
And to another, the same Spirit gives gifts of healing.
And to another the power to work miracles.
And to another the gift of prophecy.
And to another the gift to discern what the Spirit is speaking.
And to another the gift of speaking different kinds of tongues.
And to another the gift of interpretation of tongues.
Remember, it is the same Holy Spirit who distributes, activates, and operates these different gifts as He chooses for each believer.

One Body with Many Parts
Just as the human body is one, though it has many parts that together form one body, so too is Christ. For by one Spirit we all were immersed and mingled into one single body. And no matter our status – whether we are Jews or non-Jews, oppressed or free

– we are all privileged to drink deeply of the same Holy Spirit. In fact, the human body is not one single part but rather many parts mingled into one. So if the foot were to say, "Since I'm not a hand, I'm not a part of the body," it's forgetting that it is still a vital part of the body. And if the ear were to say, "Since I'm not an eye, I'm not really a part of the body," it's forgetting that it is still an important part of the body. Think of it this way. If the whole body were just an eyeball, how could it hear sounds? And if the whole body were just an ear, how could it smell different fragrances? But God has carefully designed each member and placed it in the body to function as he desires. A diversity is required, for if the body consisted of one single part, there wouldn't be a body at all! So now we see that there are many differing parts and functions, but one body.'
1 Corinthians 12:4-20 TPT

YOUR SPIRITUAL GIFTS

THE IDENTITY PROJECT

DAY 31:

YOUR SKILLS, TALENTS & PASSIONS

'I have filled him with the Spirit of God, with wisdom, with understanding, with knowledge and with all kinds of skills.'
Exodus 31:3 NIV

By now, I hope that your identity is starting to look as unique and individual as you are. Remember that God has created every part of you with great care and attention to detail. There are no accidents when it comes to the way He has put together your personality, dreams, strengths and gifts. We have one more special stone to place today in this layer of your identity as a uniquely gifted individual. This stone represents your skills, talents and passions.

I love the scripture from Exodus that opens today's reading. Let me put it into context for you. God had just used Moses powerfully to lead His people out of slavery in Egypt and they were journeying through the wilderness. At this time they were in a period of change and transition between the land where they had been slaves for 400 years and the land God had promised to them. It was during this time that God gave Moses instructions to build the 'Tent of Meeting'. This was the place that the people would come to meet with God and to worship and there were very specific guidelines about everything that was to go inside. In the middle of the instructions about exactly how everything should be built, God singles out two men from the Israelite community, Bezalel and Oholiab. He tells Moses that He has filled these two men with His Spirit and with the *wisdom*, *understanding*, *knowledge* and *skills* required to complete the tasks given. They were the men chosen and equipped by God to complete this important work. I love this and I believe that God still operates this way today.

Have you ever considered that your interests, skills, talents and passions have been placed in your life by God and actually form part of your unique identity as one of His children? I believe they were and that they actually give us great insights as to what our purpose on this Earth might be. We will look at this in more detail over the coming days, but for now, let's recognise and appreciate the truth that God has placed the skills, talents and passions we possess in each of our hearts.

This can be hard for us to get our heads around if we do not truly believe that God is good. Could it possibly be true that He has created us with our unique skills, talents and passions because He loves us and is a good Father? Could it possibly be true that when you ask God about the purpose of your life, He will not ask you to go to a deep, dark, unexplored jungle as a missionary (unless you are called and passionate about that!), but, rather, has a purpose in store for your life that beautifully uses and compliments the strengths, skills, interests and passions that He has already placed in your heart? The truth is He is that good and that the purpose He has for your life is good too!

When it comes to our skills, talents and passions, we also have the privilege of partnering with God in refining and growing our gifts. If we steward them wisely and with care, they will even open doors of opportunity for us. I love this verse from Proverbs:

> *'A man's gift makes room for him, and*
> *brings him before great men.'*
> *Proverbs 18:16*

So today, take some time to reflect on the passions of your heart. You may find your talent and passion in music, design, art, business, sport, language, discovery, people, travel, fashion, cooking, writing… or something else entirely. Whatever it is you are skilled at and passionate about, recognise these aspects of your life as gifts from God and part of your unique identity as one of His children.

PAUSE, PONDER, REFLECT

Questions to Reflect on:
What skills, talents and passions do you have? How have you invested into these areas of your life already? How have these

areas of strength and passion influenced your choices or career options? Have you ever considered that God's purpose might be in this?

Scriptures to Ponder:
> 'Keep trusting in the Lord and do what is right in his eyes.
> Fix your heart on the promises of God and you
> will be secure, feasting on his faithfulness.
> Make God the utmost delight and pleasure of your life,
> and he will provide for you what you desire the most.'
> Psalm 37:3-4 TPT

> 'We have become his poetry, a re-created people that will fulfil the destiny he has given each of us, for we are joined to Jesus, the Anointed One. Even before we were born, God planned in advance our destiny and the good works we would do to fulfil it!'
> Ephesians 2:10 TPT

> 'Every gift God freely gives us is good and perfect, streaming down from the Father of lights, who shines from the heavens with no hidden shadow or darkness and is never subject to change.' James 1:17 TPT

> 'If you are uniquely gifted in your work,
> you will rise and be promoted.
> You won't be held back—
> you'll stand before kings!'
> Proverbs 22:29 TPT

YOUR SKILLS, TALENTS & PASSIONS

THE IDENTITY PROJECT

YOUR SKILLS, TALENTS & PASSIONS

PART FOUR

positioned

FOR

purpose

- YOUR IDENTITY AS A UNIQUELY
PURPOSED INDIVIDUAL -

DAY 32:

PUTTING THE PIECES IN PLACE

'Yet you, Lord, are our Father. We are the clay, you are our potter; we are all the work of your hand.'
Isaiah 64:8 NIV

Before we dive into discovering the final layer of our identity, let's reflect on what we have discovered so far on our journey together. Hopefully the things we have discussed have become more than just interesting ideals to you over the past few weeks. It is my prayer that these seeds of truth have already begun to put down deep roots into your heart, forming a strong and solid identity that is built on the unshakable truth of what God says about who you are.

The first layer of our identity that we have built together is based on the truth that we have been created in the image of God. Each one of us has been hand made by our Creator, woven together in His likeness, and we reflect His nature in many ways. Our spirituality, creativity, intelligence, ability to communicate and relate to others, our conscience and our sense of purpose are all ways that we bear the marks of our maker. These different traits reflect aspects of God's character and in doing so, reveal the incredible value that each one of our lives have. This is the first foundation on which a strong identity is built. The truth that God has created you in His image should be the *first filter* that any thoughts you have about yourself must pass through. Anything that does not line up with the truth we have unpacked about who you are as a person created in the image of God should never be allowed to settle into your thinking patterns. You truly have been fearfully and wonderfully made!

The second layer of identity that we built together was based on the truth of who we are in Christ. Through the amazing gift of grace offered through Jesus, we, as broken and fallen people, are welcomed into the family of God. How amazing. We have spent time pondering the truth that each one of us has been chosen by God and were predestined to be found in Him. We have considered what it means for God to have redeemed us and how He declares us justified and righteous through Jesus. We have looked at how God goes even further, above and beyond anything we could ever earn or deserve by adopting us into His family as royal sons and daughters and giving us access to His glorious inheritance. And last, but certainly not least, we have looked at how God empowers us through His Holy Spirit to be a part of His story here on the Earth. Yes, the story of salvation reveals our sin, our shame and our great need for a saviour. However, it also reveals our incredible worth and value. Jesus knew and fully understood what would be required of Him in order to redeem you, and He decided you were well worth it. He went to the cross with you on His mind! You were the joy that was set before Him while He endured the torture of the crucifixion (Hebrews 12:2). The truth of who you are in Christ should be the *second filter* that any thoughts you have about yourself must pass through. Your life has great worth and value because you are a royal child of God.

The third layer of identity we have built is based on the truth that we have each been uniquely and individually created. Everything from our personality style to the gifts, strengths and passions God has placed on each of our lives point to this truth. These truths should form the *third filter* that any thoughts you have about yourself must pass through. Your life has great worth and value because you have been uniquely gifted by God for great things!

We are about to begin building the final layer of our identity, considering how all these pieces fit together perfectly in the way God has positioned our lives to achieve great purpose! Before we begin this final part of our journey, take some time to be still and reflect on the path we have already travelled together, and the truths about our identity that have already been uncovered.

PAUSE, PONDER, REFLECT

Questions to Reflect on:
As you read through this reminder of who you are, think about the way your heart responds. What truths do you feel you have started to really embrace and allowed to take root the way you see your identity? What truths are you still struggling to believe about yourself? Ask God to reveal to you lies about your identity that still need to be replaced with truth.

Scripture to Ponder:

'We look away from the natural realm and we fasten our gaze onto Jesus who birthed faith within us and who leads us forward into faith's perfection. His example is this: Because His heart was focused on the joy of knowing that you would be his, He endured the agony of the cross and conquered its humiliation, and now sits exalted at the right hand of the throne of God!'
Hebrews 12:2 TPT

"Your lives are like salt among the people. But if you, like salt, become bland, how can your 'saltiness' be restored? Flavorless salt is good for nothing and will be thrown out and trampled on by others. "Your lives light up the world. Let others see your light from a distance, for how can you hide a city that stands on a hilltop? And who would light a lamp and then hide it in an obscure place? Instead, it's placed where everyone in the house can benefit from its light. So don't hide your light! Let it shine brightly before others, so that the commendable things you do will shine as light upon them, and then they will give their praise to your Father in heaven."
Matthew 5:13-16 TPT

"For my thoughts are not your thoughts,
neither are your ways my ways," declares the Lord.
"As the heavens are higher than the earth,
so are my ways higher than your ways
and my thoughts than your thoughts.
As the rain and the snow
come down from heaven,

*and do not return to it
without watering the earth
and making it bud and flourish,
so that it yields seed for the sower and bread for the eater,
so is my word that goes out from my mouth:
It will not return to me empty,
but will accomplish what I desire
and achieve the purpose for which I sent it."
Isaiah 55:8-11 NIV*

PUTTING THE PIECES IN PLACE

THE IDENTITY PROJECT

DAY 33:

DISCOVERING PURPOSE

'For I know the plans I have for you,' declares the Lord, 'plans to prosper you and not to harm you, plans to give you hope and a future.'
Jeremiah 29:11 NIV

I have said it before in this journal and I just feel that I need to say it again. I believe with my whole heart that if you truly understood God's plan for your life you wouldn't want to be anyone other than the person He created you to be! If you could glimpse for a moment the future He has intended for you – a future that is tailor made to suit your unique strengths, skills and passions, a future full of hope and promise, and a future full of fun and adventure – any insecurities you felt about who you are would vanish instantly.

However, as wonderful as it would be to fast-forward life and glimpse this moment, we are called to live each day by faith. We are called to believe and to stand on God's promises to us, even when we cannot see how things will come together. We are called to trust and to listen to the voice of God's goodness and faithfulness rather than our fears and doubts. The author of the book of Hebrews describes faith beautifully:

> *'Now faith is confidence in what we hope for and*
> *assurance about what we do not see.'*
> Hebrews 11:1 NIV

You, my friend, are called to walk with *confidence* and *assurance* that God's plan and purpose for your life is good and that it will come to pass, even when you cannot see how or when it might happen. That is what it means to walk by faith.

Now, while we may not get to see the master plan or the big picture of how everything will come together for us, God does invite us into His purpose and loves to reveal His plan to us step by step. Remember, He is a good Father who He loves to lead His children into His best for their lives. Look at the following scriptures that promise God's leading:

> *'I will instruct you and teach you in the way you should go;*
> *I will counsel you with my loving eye upon you.' Psalm 32:8 NIV*

> *'Whether you turn to the right or to the left, your ears will hear*
> *a voice behind you, saying, "This is the way; walk in it."'*
> Isaiah 30:21 NIV

How comforting to know that as we walk this journey of faith, God is right alongside us guiding our steps. I have found that when it comes to discovering purpose in our lives, God has already placed many insights and signs within our hearts that point us in the direction we are meant to go. We have looked at some of the ways that God has uniquely designed and created each one of us over the past few days. Today we will begin to pull these together under the banner of purpose.

I have three questions for you to consider that I believe may help you begin to discern purpose for your life:

1. What do you love? What gets you out of bed every morning? What makes you come alive? What do you love to do?

2. What do you hate? What things can you absolutely not stand? What injustices or inequalities in the world really get under your skin?

3. What are you good at? Look back at your thoughts from a few days ago. What strengths, talents, skills, abilities and passions do you have?

I believe that for most of us, true purpose and fulfilment in our lives will be a combination of the answers to these questions. This is where we find our 'sweet spot' in life; a place where we feel empowered, passionate and like our lives are truly making a difference.

PAUSE, PONDER, REFLECT

Questions to Reflect on:
Consider the questions above and write down your honest

responses. Do you see a pattern of purpose in your thoughts? Do you see a way that the things you love and the things that you are most passionate about could come together to bring change to the things you hate in the world? Could this be a clue to the purpose God has for your life?

Scripture to Ponder:

> 'Then I heard the voice of the Lord saying, "Whom shall I send? And who will go for us?" And I said, "Here am I. Send me!" '
> Isaiah 6:8 NIV

> 'For if you remain silent at this time, relief and deliverance for the Jews will arise from another place, but you and your father's family will perish. And who knows but that you have come to your royal position for such a time as this?'
> Esther 4:14 NIV

> 'So here's what I want you to do, God helping you: Take your everyday, ordinary life—your sleeping, eating, going-to-work, and walking-around life—and place it before God as an offering. Embracing what God does for you is the best thing you can do for Him. Don't become so well-adjusted to your culture that you fit into it without even thinking. Instead, fix your attention on God. You'll be changed from the inside out. Readily recognize what He wants from you, and quickly respond to it. Unlike the culture around you,

always dragging you down to its level of immaturity, God brings the best out of you, develops well-formed maturity in you.'
Romans 12:1-2 MSG

THE IDENTITY PROJECT

DISCOVERING PURPOSE

DAY 34:

WRITE IT DOWN

'Write the vision and make it plain on tablets, that he may run who reads it. For the vision is yet for an appointed time; but at the end it will speak, and it will not lie. Though it tarries, wait for it; because it will surely come'
Habakkuk 2:2-3 NKJV

In the book of Habakkuk, God gave a prophetic word to the prophet Habakkuk. Yep, that was his name. God instructed him to write down the vision that he had seen so that it could be carried by a messenger. The message was too important to be lost or forgotten. I feel that the same is true when it comes to your identity. The work we have done together over the last few weeks in uncovering who you are based on the truth of God's word is far too precious to be forgotten or lost. It needs to be written down.

God also cautioned Habakkuk to wait for the message to come to pass, saying that the vision was for an appointed time. Even if it took a while, even if it didn't look like things were going to happen, God's instruction was to wait, trusting that He would bring the vision to pass at the perfect time. Sounds like living by faith!

There is something so powerful about what Habakkuk did in writing down the vision he had seen. Putting our beliefs, hopes, dreams and visions for the future down in writing is just as powerful for us today. Something happens within us when we give the desires of our hearts enough acknowledgement and attention that they can be transferred from thoughts and feelings into words on a page. They become clearer through this process and the next steps towards achieving them often become more obvious to us.

I love *The Message* translation of the verse above. When speaking of the vision it says *'Write it down. Write it out in big block letters so that it can be seen on the run.'* (Hab 2:2-3) Today, we are going to begin doing just that! We are going to put everything we have unpacked over the last few weeks together on one page – something that you can keep coming back to, something that can continually remind you of who you are and the purpose God has for your life. By the end of this activity you should have a complete 'Identity Board' that you can display somewhere in your space to remind you of who you are according to the Word of God.

If you head online to www.identityproject.com.au you will find a free downloadable template for an identity board that you can use to complete this activity. The idea is that this board will become a reflection of your unique and individual identity. You will see that there are spaces on this template for you to record specific details about the way God has created you, as well as plenty of blank space. Use these spaces as freely as you want to. You may want to write down dreams and goals that you have, prophetic words that have been spoken over your life, your favourite scriptures, or positive affirmations. Be as creative as you would like to be!

In fact, feel free to create your own unique board design if you want to. This activity may take you a few days, even a few weeks to complete, and you might find yourself still adding things to it months down the track – and that is totally okay. I do encourage you, however, to do enough over the next two days that you can hang your Identity Board somewhere in your space where you can see it often and can begin to reflect on it – somewhere that it can be *seen on the run*!

Also available for you to download for free from www.identityproject.com.au are a some sets of identity affirmation cards. Why not take some time today to print these and strategically place them around your space so that you can be reminded every time you see them of your true identity. By 'strategically,' I mean place them in spots that you are likely to be confronted by old thoughts about who you are. Perhaps stuck on the bathroom mirror – hello! Or inside your wardrobe… for when you are having those days where you feel like you don't look good in anything! Other good spots to place them are areas where you often find yourself with time to think so that you can meditate on the truth of their words. Perhaps in your car if you are a driver (I always have a positive quote or scripture tucked into my sun visor), or on your bedside table where you will see it as you go to bed each night. Have fun with this and get creative.

PAUSE, PONDER, REFLECT

Thoughts to Reflect on:
Use this space to begin to gather your thoughts and dreams before transferring them to your Identity Board. Please do not feel confined to the space contained in this journal. Include images, pictures, photos, bright colours, even glitter if you would like to. Your identity poster should be as unique and individual as you are.

Scriptures to Ponder:

'And then God answered: "Write this.
Write what you see.
Write it out in big block letters
so that it can be read on the run.
This vision-message is a witness
pointing to what's coming.
It aches for the coming—it can hardly wait!
And it doesn't lie.
If it seems slow in coming, wait.
It's on its way. It will come right on time.'
Habakkuk 2:2-3 MSG

'I will pour out my Spirit
on every kind of people:
Your sons will prophesy,
also your daughters.

*Your old men will dream,
your young men will see visions.'*
Joel 2:28 MSG

'Now may God, the inspiration and fountain of hope, fill you to overflowing with uncontainable joy and perfect peace as you trust in Him. And may the power of the Holy Spirit continually surround your life with his super-abundance until you radiate with hope!'
Romans 15:13 TPT

WRITE IT DOWN

THE IDENTITY PROJECT

DAY 35:

PEARLS & PIGS

'Do not give dogs what is sacred; do not throw your pearls to pigs. If you do, they may trample them under their feet, and turn and tear you to pieces.'
Matthew 7:6 NIV

I trust that you let all your creative energy loose yesterday in beginning to build an Identity Board that reflects how uniquely and individually you have been created! I pray that as you display that board in a special place, it becomes a continual source of encouragement to your spirit, reminding you always of who you are and the value and worth your life has simply because you belong to God.

Today I would like to look at the words of Jesus in Matthew 7 and give you a word of caution when it comes to protecting your identity, your dreams and your sense of purpose. As we have discovered over the last few weeks, you are incredibly and unconditionally loved by a God who was so passionate about you that His son, Jesus, went to the cross so that you could be welcomed completely into His family. This love will never change. It is constant. It is secure. It is extravagant and it is extreme. It is a love that can heal all wounds and restore all things that have been broken. It is a love that can ignite dreams and purpose in your heart and sustain you through challenges. You, my friend, are utterly and completely loved!

While God's love will never disappoint you or let you down, other people will. I am sure that at some time in your life you have experienced pain, disappointment and hurt from other relationships in your world. It is important to recognise that ultimately we do not fight and struggle against other people, but against powers of darkness and spiritual forces of evil (Ephesians 6:12). The truth is you are deeply loved by a God who has an enemy. Although he is no match for the Almighty God and will soon be completely defeated (Revelation 20), at the moment he tries his best to hurt the heart of God by hurting those who belong to Him, and often he will use other people to do this, sometimes without them even realising.

In Matthew 7:6, Jesus gives what appears to be some strange advice to those listening to him about dogs, pearls and pigs. He says not to give dogs things that are sacred and not to throw your pearls to pigs. Put in other words, do not give things of great significance or value to people who do not understand or appreciate them. Why? Jesus says they may trample them under their feet and then turn and tear you to pieces.

Now, we aren't talking about literal dogs and pigs here, but have you ever been in a situation where you went out on a limb to share something significant about your life, only to have your words trampled by those you shared it with? Perhaps it was a dream, an idea, an opinion or an experience. You extended a pearl, to use the analogy Jesus did, and rather than it being recognised or valued, it was crushed. It is a horrible feeling that can leave you feeling like you have been ripped to shreds. The most challenging part about a situation like this is that sometimes the people who have hurt you may not even realise what has happened or the impact of their words and actions.

So, what does this have to do with our purpose, dreams and visions for the future? A lot! Please, my friend, be careful who you share these valuable and significant pearls with. Remember that your dreams are precious and use wisdom when choosing how to share them. The enemy would love nothing more than to crush them before they begin to bloom, robbing the world of the beauty and hope that they hold. On the other hand, sharing your dreams with people of faith who can be trusted in this area can be one of the greatest and most rewarding experiences, not hindering your dreams but propelling them forward.

PAUSE, PONDER, REFLECT

Questions to Reflect on:
Have you experienced pain when sharing your hopes or dreams with people in the past? Ask God to heal your heart and help you to forgive those who have hurt you. Who do you have around your life now that you are likely to share your dreams with? Place

these people before God and ask for wisdom about if, how and when to share your pearls.

Scriptures to Ponder:
> 'My child, if you truly want a long and satisfying life,
> never forget the things that I've taught you.
> Follow closely every truth that I've given you.
> Then you will have a full, rewarding life.
> Hold on to loyal love and don't let go,
> and be faithful to all that you've been taught.
> Let your life be shaped by integrity,
> with truth written upon your heart.
> That's how you will find favor and understanding
> with both God and men—
> you will gain the reputation of living life well.
> Trust in the Lord completely,
> and do not rely on your own opinions.
> With all your heart rely on Him to guide you,
> and He will lead you in every decision you make.
> Become intimate with him in whatever you do,
> and He will lead you wherever you go.
> Don't think for a moment that you know it all,
> for wisdom comes when you adore him with undivided devotion
> and avoid everything that's wrong.
> Then you will find the healing refreshment
> your body and spirit long for.'
> Proverbs 3:1-8 TPT

PEARLS & PIGS

THE IDENTITY PROJECT

PEARLS & PIGS

PART FIVE

building

HEALTHY

habits

- CREATING AN ENVIRONMENT
OF STRENGTH AND GROWTH -

DAY 36:

READING THE WORD

'Blessed is the one ... whose delight is in the law of the Lord, and who meditates on His law day and night. That person is like a tree planted by streams of water, which yields its fruit in season, and whose leaf does not wither - whatever they do prospers.'
Psalm 1:1-3 NIV

We are nearing the end of our journey together! I hope you have enjoyed our time discovering the truth of what God thinks about you and I hope that the way you see and value yourself today is closer to the way God sees and values you than it might have been a few weeks ago.

Before we finish this journey, I wanted to leave you with some practical daily habits that will help to keep your identity and self-image strong and healthy. Just as a young seedling will grow and flourish more in an environment where it receives the water, sunlight and nutrients it needs each day, your identity and the way you see yourself will grow stronger, and become truly established in your heart, if it is kept in the right environment.

The first element needed to keep your identity strong and

grounded is the Word of God – the Bible. Everything we have unpacked in the last few weeks about identity has come from the Word of God. It is the truth of God's word that has broken down the negative images of ourselves that we have constructed and it is the truth of God's words that has built a new, whole and restored self-image in their place. It is absolutely necessary that His words continue to be a part of our daily lives in order for our identities to remain strong.

Psalm 1 gives a beautiful picture of the person who reads and meditates on the Word of God being like a tree planted by streams of water – its roots are deep, its branches bear fruit, it is not swayed by storms and continues to grow whatever the circumstances. I don't know about you, but that sounds like an awesome picture of what life can be like! So, let's look at how we can make reading and meditating on the Word of God a daily part of our lives.

Firstly, reading the word everyday is not something that will happen in your life by accident. You have to prioritise it, make time for it and be intentional about building this habit. You also have to be prepared for the 100 things you have to do that will suddenly come to mind the moment you start to read. But, if you don't already, I challenge you to set some time aside each day to read the Bible. Get creative, make a plan and persevere to stick with it!

If you're not sure where to start, go to the Gospels – the books of Matthew, Mark, Luke and John. They are recounts of the things Jesus said and did while on Earth. Proverbs is also a great book to read daily. There are 31 chapters – one for every day of the month – and it is full of wisdom that can be applied to daily life. If you are struggling for time, take advantage of some of the amazing technology currently available to us. There are great audio translations out there - you can listen to the Bible in your car, on your way to work or while you are at the gym. There are also great apps available to read the Bible on your phone or tablet. You can literally take God's Word with you in your pocket everywhere you go!

If you are still really struggling, try experimenting with a different version of the Bible. You might find The Message Translation or The Passion Translation, for example, easier to read daily than the King James Version. The authors of these translations have spent a great deal of time and effort studying and cross checking to ensure God's message is communicated with accuracy and integrity in these translations, but in language we use everyday.

Finally, after making time and space in your life to read the Bible everyday, make time to meditate, reflect, and think deeply about the words that you have read. You might do this by choosing one verse everyday to commit to memory and pondering how you can apply that word to your life as you memorise it. You might do this by writing down a verse that stands out to you as you read, and then journaling what it means to you personally. You might do this by selecting a verse and looking at where the key words from that verse appear in other parts of the Bible. However you choose to meditate on the Word of God, the goal is that the scriptures you have read become more than just words on a page, but words that come alive and carry deep meaning that can change and transform your thinking and actions.

The most beautiful thing that takes place as we read the Word of God each day is that we learn who God is in a deeper and more personal way. His words reveal His character, His love and His promises. As we read we grow in our knowledge of Him and our love for Him at the same time. Make a decision today to prioritise the word of God in your life.

PAUSE, PONDER, REFLECT

Questions to Reflect on:
What are the current patterns and habits in your life around reading and meditating on the Word of God? What things might you like to change in this area? How do you think you will do this practically? If you are looking for some apps to use to help you read scripture, head to our online community at www.identityproject.com.au.

Scriptures to Ponder:
'But as for you, continue in what you have learned and have become convinced of, because you know those from whom you learned it, and how from infancy you have known the Holy Scriptures, which are able to make you wise for salvation through faith in Christ Jesus.

All Scripture is God-breathed and is useful for teaching, rebuking, correcting and training in righteousness, so that the servant of God may be thoroughly equipped for every good work.'
2 Timothy 3:14-17 NIV

'For we have the living Word of God, which is full of energy, and it pierces more sharply than a two-edged sword. It will even penetrate to the very core of our being where soul and spirit, bone and marrow meet! It interprets and reveals the true thoughts and secret motives of our hearts. There is not one person who can hide their thoughts from God, for nothing that we do remains a secret, and nothing created is concealed, but everything is exposed and defenseless before his eyes, to whom we must render an account.'
Hebrews 4:12-13 TPT

'The grass withers and the flowers fall, but the Word of our God endures forever.'
Isaiah 40:8 NIV

READING THE WORD

THE IDENTITY PROJECT

DAY 37:

PRAYER

*'But when you pray, go into your room, close the door
and pray to your Father, who is unseen. Then your Father,
who sees what is done in secret, will reward you.'*
Matthew 6:6 NIV

The second element needed to keep your identity strong and healthy is a vibrant prayer life. Whatever you have heard or thought about prayer, I want to encourage you that it isn't complicated and it isn't difficult, boring or something that you *must do* to be a good follower of Jesus. The call to pray is actually a personal invitation to embark on a great adventure with God and I want to encourage to you be making the most of the incredible opportunity you have been given to communicate with God through prayer. Let's take some time today to clarify a few things about what prayer *is* and what prayer *isn't*.

Prayer isn't a performance; it is connection.
It is important to remember that the God you are praying to sees you all the time and hears you all the time. He sees you on your good days and He sees you on your bad days, He even sees you on your ugly days. He sees it all, He hears it all! God is not fooled

for a minute when you pray to Him pretending to be someone you are not. He is also not fooled when you pray to Him like everything is okay in your world when it's not. He is not impressed when you pray to Him using fancy words or phrases when you honestly don't even know what they mean, but He *is* impressed when you show up simply and honestly to just spend time with Him.

Prayer is not a performance. Prayer is connection. It is the realisation that no matter what you are going through, you can connect anytime and anywhere with God, your Father in Heaven, and the Lord Most High. He is the one who created the Heavens and the Earth, who holds the stars in His hands, and who knows the beginning from the end. He is the one who promises to work all things together for the good of those who love Him. And do you know what? He is okay with things being a bit messy. He is okay with things being a bit real.

Our relationship with God is not meant to be filtered. He doesn't need you to try crop out the messy bits or make it appear like you have it all together when you come to Him. He wants you to come to Him as you are, openly and honestly, and connect with Him.

Prayer isn't a formula; it is a conversation.
In the same way that God is not looking for a performance, He is not looking for a practiced ritual or meaningless words either. God wants your prayer life to be real. He wants it to be authentic. He wants it to be genuine. He wants it to be honest. He wants it

to be open — and do you know what else? He wants to be in on the conversation! How's that for a thought. When you come to talk to God, He actually wants to talk to you too! I will share with you in more detail about how to hear the voice of God in the next few days.

Prayer isn't a wish list; it is an opportunity to partner with God.
Yes, prayer is an opportunity to invite God into our world. It's an opportunity to connect and communicate with Him anytime and anywhere about whatever we are going through. But did you know that the partnership of prayer goes both ways? Prayer is also God's opportunity to invite us into His world. Did you know that He wants to partner with you in bringing Heaven to Earth? He does! He want's you to be a part of His Kingdom being shown on the Earth and His will being done in and through our lives. Doesn't this sound like the greatest adventure you could ever embark on?

I encourage you to stay connected to your Heavenly Father everyday through prayer. It will help to remind you who your father is, and who you are as His precious child. This is the living truth that your identity and self image needs to be consistently anchored to.

PAUSE, PONDER, REFLECT

Questions to Reflect on:

Take some time today to honestly evaluate your prayer life. How often do you connect with God throughout the day in prayer? How often do you stop to invite Him into your conversations or decisions? How can you make an effort to connect with God more frequently? Take some time to stop and connect with God right now.

Scriptures to Ponder:

'Do not be anxious about anything, but in every situation, by prayer and petition, with thanksgiving, present your requests to God.'
Philippians 4:6 NIV

'And when you come before God, don't turn that into a theatrical production either. All these people making a regular show out of their prayers, hoping for stardom! Do you think God sits in a box seat? Here's what I want you to do: Find a quiet, secluded place so you won't be tempted to role-play before God. Just be there as simply and honestly as you can manage. The focus will shift from you to God, and you will begin to sense his grace. The world is full of so-called prayer warriors who are prayer-ignorant. They're full of formulas and programs and advice, peddling techniques for getting what you want from God. Don't fall for that nonsense. This is your Father you are dealing with, and He knows better than you what you need. With a God like this loving you, you can pray very simply.'
Matthew 6:5-7 MSG

PRAYER

'This, then, is how you should pray:
Our Father in heaven,
hallowed be your name,
your kingdom come,
your will be done,
on earth as it is in heaven.
Give us today our daily bread.
And forgive us our debts,
as we also have forgiven our debtors.
And lead us not into temptation,
but deliver us from the evil one.'
Matthew 6:5-13 NIV

THE IDENTITY PROJECT

PRAYER

DAY 38:

WORSHIP

'Seek the Lord and His strength; seek His presence continually!' 2 Chronicles 16:11 ESV

The third habit to develop in your life if you want to keep your identity strong and healthy is one of worship. As we will discover together today, worship is powerful. Worship shifts our focus and attention away from ourselves and onto God, where it rightfully belongs. Worship reminds us who God is, and also who we are as His children. When we are facing challenging circumstances, worship puts things back into perspective, and by ushering us into God's presence, worship brings us into a place of greater intimacy with our Father in Heaven. Let's unpack a few thoughts around worship together.

What is worship?
We can easily fall into the trap of thinking that worship is limited to the songs we sing to God at church on Sundays. While singing is a wonderful expression of worship, there is so much more to worship than singing alone. I love the way that Webster's Dictionary defines the word worship as *'To honour with extravagant love and extreme submission.'*[8] I think this definition captures so

beautifully the truth that worship is really about our hearts, and developing a deep desire within us to love, honour and submit to God. This heart attitude of worship can be expressed in many different ways. Through song, through words, through actions and through choices, we can express love and honour to God in worship. This was what the Apostle Paul was referring to when he encouraged the Romans to place their whole lives before God as an act of worship (Romans 12:1). I love *The Message* translation of this scripture:

'So here's what I want you to do, God helping you: Take your everyday, ordinary life—your sleeping, eating, going-to-work, and walking-around life—and place it before God as an offering.' Romans 12:1 MSG

Worship can be extended to every corner of our lives. Even the most boring and mundane tasks can become acts of worship when they are done with a heart overflowing with love for God, and a desire to honour Him in every word and action.

An attitude of gratitude
So, on a practical level, how do we develop habits of worship in our lives? I have found one of the simplest, yet most powerful ways to build a life of worship is to develop an attitude of gratefulness and thanksgiving. Just as the writer of Psalm 100 instructed the people of Israel to approach God with songs of thankfulness and praise, I have found it is still the quickest way into God's presence today. When we begin to think about, speak aloud or sing out the good things God has done for us, and the things we are thankful

for, we lift up worship to our Father in Heaven and invite His presence into our lives.

Communion
Another aspect of worship that I have found to be so powerful in my own life is the act of taking communion. Jesus instituted this beautiful practice when He ate with His disciples for the last time before going to the cross. When He broke the bread and shared the wine with those closest to Him that night, His words were so simple: 'Remember me' (Matthew 26:26-29). Pausing in the midst of the business of life to remember Jesus and what He accomplished for us on the cross is so powerful. The elements of bread and juice remind us of the way that Jesus body was broken and His blood was shed. They speak of the freedom and victory of the cross and the price that was paid to win that freedom. These simple elements also proclaim the continuing triumph of the cross in our lives today. Whenever I hold these elements in my hands I cannot help but be overcome with gratitude, thankfulness and worship for what my saviour has done for me.

However you choose to connect with God in worship, the best thing about it is that you can do it anywhere – in the car, at work, in the shower – you don't need a band or a choir in order to worship God. You can pause and take a moment to be grateful and thank Him for the good things He has done in your life anywhere. You can stop and remind yourself of who He is and what He has done for you at any point throughout your day. And you can worship Him by seeking to love and honour Him not only with your words, but with your actions, choices and thoughts!

I encourage you to connect everyday with your Heavenly Father through worship.

PAUSE, PONDER, REFLECT

Take some time today to worship God. You might want to put on some music, write in your journal or just use your words. Bring Him words of thanks and praise, meditate on the good things He has done for you and declare your love for Him. Ask God to help you build a greater atmosphere of worship around your life.

A large part of worship is obedience. Is there anything God has asked you to do recently that you have been putting off or procrastinating about? Perhaps a phone call you need to make, or some words that need to be said in a relationship. Don't wait any longer!

Scriptures to Ponder:

'Therefore, since we are receiving a kingdom that cannot be shaken, let us be thankful, and so worship God acceptably with reverence and awe, for our "God is a consuming fire." '
Romans 12:28-29 NIV

'Lift up a great shout of joy to the Lord!
Go ahead and do it—everyone, everywhere!
As you serve Him, be glad and worship Him.
Sing your way into His presence with joy!
And realize what this really means—
we have the privilege of worshiping the Lord our God.

For He is our Creator and we belong to Him.
We are the people of His pleasure.
You can pass through His open gates with the password of praise.
Come right into His presence with thanksgiving.
Come bring your thank offering to Him
and affectionately bless His beautiful name!
For the Lord is always good and ready to receive you.
He's so loving that it will amaze you—
so kind that it will astound you!
And He is famous for his faithfulness toward all.
Everyone knows our God can be trusted,
for He keeps his promises to every generation!'
Psalm 100 TPT

WORSHIP

THE IDENTITY PROJECT

DAY 39:
HEARING GOD'S VOICE

'Whether you turn to the right or to the left, your ears will hear a voice behind you, saying, "This is the way; walk in it."' Isaiah 30:21 NIV

Today we will look at the final element necessary to keep your identity and self-image strong and grounded in truth – the discipline of recognising and listening to God's voice. I don't know about you, but I am so glad we don't serve a silent God! No, Our God is a speaking God. He created the world with words, He is still speaking today and He wants to speak to you personally. How amazing is that!

Before we look at some of the different ways that God might choose to speak to us, let's look at a few quick checks that you should run any word from God through before acting on it. These checks should be applied to things you feel God is speaking to your heart personally, as well as words of prophecy or encouragement that you receive from others.

1. Anything God speaks to you will be in line with His Word.
God is constant and consistent. He does not change or contradict Himself. No true word that He speaks to your heart or through someone else will contradict the truth that He has revealed to us in the Bible.

2. Anything God speaks to you will be in line with His Character.
Once again, God does not change. He is consistent. He is still faithful and just, still merciful and kind and He is still loving. A word from God will be in line with His character as revealed in the Bible and in our own lives.

Any time that God speaks to you it will be within these parameters. This doesn't mean that a word from God won't put you in a place that is little bit confronting, a little bit scary or a little bit outside of your comfort zone! However, even when God needs to pull us into line, He will always bring His message of truth in a loving way.

So, let's get practical. How can we hear God's voice? I love the way that author and speaker Havilah Cunnington articulates the different ways that God speaks to us, and we will explore these together today[9]. There are, in fact, four different and distinct ways that God is seen to communicate with people throughout the Bible, and I believe that God communicates to us in these same ways today. Let's look at them together.

A Knowing... Often in the scriptures, God speaks to people through discernment, and He still does today. This can be best described as a deep knowing within your spirit of what you need to do or what God is saying to you. This inner knowing goes beyond your own wisdom, understanding or knowledge, and comes with a sense of peace. It is a spiritual discernment. If you hear from God in this way you might find that you can walk through challenging or difficult situations with a deep confidence that God has got things covered.

This might sound like:
- 'I just *know* that this is the decision we need to make…'
- 'I just have a *strong sense of peace* about going this way…'
- 'I have *a great confidence* that God is with us in this…'

Examples in the Scriptures:
- John 21:12-13 After Jesus had been resurrected He saw the disciples and called to them to come and have breakfast with Him. The scriptures say that none of them needed to ask Him who He was, for they all *knew* it was the Lord.
- Luke 10: 38-39 Mary *knew* she just needed to sit at Jesus feet when He came to the house.
- 2 Chronicles 1 King Solomon chose to ask God for great *wisdom* and *discernment*.

A Hearing…Many times in the scriptures, God speaks to people through a voice, and you may hear Him speak to you in this way too. This voice can sometimes be heard audibly, or silently within your spirit. It is almost like you hear a voice or thought in your mind that you know is not your own. Once again, God's word is accompanied by a sense of peace. People who hear God in this way may find they are able to navigate challenges in life without loosing their peace by standing on a specific word or promise that they have heard from God.

This might sound like:
> 'I was praying and God said this to me…'
> 'I just heard the Holy Spirit say…'
> 'The promise for us in this situation is…'

Examples in the Scriptures:
- 1 Samuel 3 When Samuel was a young boy he heard the voice of God calling to him.
- Isaiah 30:21 When you turn to the right or to the left your ears will hear a voice behind you, saying, 'This is the way, walk in it.'

A Seeing… Many times in the Bible, and still today, God speaks through visions and pictures. These may come in the form of dreams, images in your minds eye or visions that you see in the spirit. Again, they are pictures that you know are beyond your own imaginations, and often a message or meaning accompanies them. People who hear from God in this way are often great dreamers, and are able to see how things should be or could be. Able to hang onto a picture of what God is going to do.

This might sound like:
> 'God showed me a picture of us on the other side of this…'
> 'I had a vision of us doing this together…'
> 'I had a dream that you were…'

Examples in the Scriptures:
- Acts 10 Peter receives a vision that commissioned him to

preach to the gentiles.
- Acts 16 Paul has a vision in the night of a man from Macedonia was standing and appealing to him, and saying, 'Come over to Macedonia and help us.'
- Matthew 2 Joseph has a dream where God instructs him to flee to Egypt with Mary and Jesus.

A Feeling... The fourth way that God speaks to people in the Bible and today is through feelings. This can best be described as experiencing feelings or emotions that go beyond what you would naturally feel or experience at a certain time or in a certain place. It is as if God allows you to feel His heart in a situation or about a person.

This might sound like:
> 'As soon as I walked into the room I suddenly felt...'
> 'When I saw you today I just felt really sad/ worried/ joyful...'
> 'I felt a heaviness/ peace/ sadness come over me when I started to pray for you...'

Examples in the Scriptures:
- Many of the prophets were people who felt the heart of God for His people. Sometimes great sadness, sometimes great joy.

The Bible... One more way that God may speak to you is through the words He has already given to us – the Bible. There have been countless times in my life when the words of scripture have spoken so specifically and directly to a situation I was facing, that it felt like God had written the verse just for me! The book of Hebrews describes the word of God as living and active (Hebrews 4:12), and it certainly is! When you read it you can expect God to speak to you.

God may choose to speak to you in any, or all of these different ways. What is most important for us to do is make sure that we are always positioned to hear His voice, not only for ourselves, but for others in our lives. Keep the lines of communication open and expect to hear from God each day.

PAUSE, PONDER, REFLECT

Think about times in your life when God has spoken to you. How did He communicate? Ask God to speak to you today and spend time waiting on Him. Write down anything you hear Him saying to your heart.

Scriptures to Ponder:
'For the word of God is alive and active. Sharper than any double-edged sword, it penetrates even to dividing soul and spirit, joints and marrow; it judges the thoughts and attitudes of the heart. Nothing in all creation is hidden from God's sight. Everything is uncovered and laid bare before the eyes of Him to whom we must give account.'
Hebrews 4:12-13 NIV

HEARING GOD'S VOICE

'Jesus answered, "It is written: 'Man shall not live on bread alone, but on every word that comes from the mouth of God.' " Matthew 4:4 NIV

'My own sheep will hear my voice and I know each one, and they will follow me.' John 10:27 TPT

THE IDENTITY PROJECT

HEARING GOD'S VOICE

DAY 40:

GO & LIVE LOVED!

*'Beloved, I pray that you may prosper in all things
and be in health, just as your soul prospers.'*
3 John 2 NKJV

Wow! We have reached a very significant milestone today – the end of a 40 day journey together discovering and building a strong and solid identity! I trust that God has done some construction work in your heart over the past few weeks to bring you to a place of security in who you are in Him.

Over the last few days we have spent some time considering the kind of environment that is required for our identity to remain strong and firmly grounded in the truth of God's word. Each of the elements we have looked at compliment and work hand in hand with each other. As you begin to read and study the Bible more frequently, it should prompt you to want to dialogue and connect with God personally in prayer. The more you connect with God through prayer, the more worship should begin to bubble up in your heart. And the more time you spend in God's presence through prayer and worship, the easier it should become for you to recognise and hear God's voice in your own life.

None of these habits is designed to be religious tasks to check off each day, or things you need to do to please God. In fact, they are the complete opposite! They are simply disciplines that should help to cultivate a vibrant, intimate and personal relationship with God. The kind of relationship God longs for you to have with him. You are not designed to navigate this life alone, and you do not have to. Your loving Father wants to guide you every step of the way, helping you walk in divine destiny and purpose, and reminding you of your worth and value along the way, should you happen to loose sight of it.

My deepest desire for you, as you continue your great adventure with God, is that this would be only the beginning of a life that grows and flourishes like a well planted tree. I pray that whatever storms come your way, your roots will continue to be established in the truth of who you are.

Remember, my friend, that you have been fearfully and wonderfully made. You are deeply loved and your life has great value. You have been marked by your Maker, and created in the image of God. You have been redeemed through the cross, welcomed into God's family and are now found in Christ. You have been uniquely and individually gifted for great things – there is no one else like you! And you have been strategically positioned for purpose, dreams and destiny. Go and live loved! My prayer for you as we part ways is the prayer that Paul prayed for the Ephesian church:

'For this reason I kneel before the Father, from whom every family in

heaven and on earth derives its name. I pray that out of His glorious riches He may strengthen you with power through His Spirit in your inner being, so that Christ may dwell in your hearts through faith. And I pray that you, being rooted and established in love, may have power, together with all the Lord's holy people, to grasp how wide and long and high and deep is the love of Christ, and to know this love that surpasses knowledge—that you may be filled to the measure of all the fullness of God. Now to Him who is able to do immeasurably more than all we ask or imagine, according to His power that is at work within us, to Him be glory in the church and in Christ Jesus throughout all generations, for ever and ever! Amen'. Ephesians 3:14-21

PAUSE, PONDER, REFLECT

'Be still, and know that I am God.' Psalm 46:10 NKJV

Reflect and be still in God's presence today. Take some time today to think back over the last 40 days. What have been the most significant changes in your thinking? What truths have been easy to work into your identity? What truths have been challenging to embrace? What is the next step for you as you journey with Jesus through life?

GO & LIVE LOVED!

THE IDENTITY PROJECT

THANKYOU

Aaron, thank you for always being my biggest encourager and my best friend.

Jilly, Kaz & Lynette, I could never thank you enough for the time you put into this manuscript. You are all incredible gifts to my life.

The amazing tribe of women that surround my life, I could not possibly name you all here, but you are a constant source of life and hope to me. I thank God for you everyday,

James, Nicole, Natalie and the team at Ark House Press. Without you this dream would have never left my macbook.

And finally, Jesus Christ, my everything. This book is a gift from you, surrendered back to you for your glory.

REFERENCES

1. Staub, D (2010). *About You.* San Francisco, CA: Jossey-Bass

2. Elwell, W A (1996). Entry for 'Redeem, Redemption'. Evangelical *Dictionary of Theology.* Retrieved June 28, 2018, from https://www.biblestudytools.com/dictionary/redeem-redemption/

3. Justify 1344 [Def] (n.d.) Strongs Greek Concordance. Retrieved June 28, 2018, from http://biblehub.com/str/greek/1344.htm

4. Ashby, C (2016). Adoption in the Roman Empire. Retrieved from https://carolashby.com/adoption-in-the-roman-empire/

5. Parke, B (2018). The Wonderful Implications of God being Abba Father. Retrieved from https://www.biblestudytools.com/bible-study/topical-studies/the-wonderful-implications-of-god-being-our-abba-father.html

6. Encyclopedia Britannica (2018). Wonder Woman. Retrieved July 5, 2018 from https://www.britannica.com/topic/Wonder-Woman#ref1069002

7. Chapman, G (2010). *The Five Love Langauges. The Secret to Love that Lasts.* Chicago, IL: Northfield Publishing.

8. Worship [Def. 3] (n.d.) Webster's Dictionary Online Edition. Retrieved July 10, 2018, from http://webstersdictionary1828.com/Dictionary/worship

9. Cunnington, H (2019). *Prophetic Personalities*. Online Course Workbook. Retrieved April 10, 2019 from https://truthtotable.com/prophetic-personalities/

www.ingramcontent.com/pod-product-compliance
Lightning Source LLC
LaVergne TN
LVHW051514070426
835507LV00023B/3114